TEACHING MOTIVES FOR WRITING

An Instructor's Manual to Accompany Motives for Writing

Sally Barr Reagan
University of Missouri, St. Louis

Mayfield Publishing Company
Mountain View, California
London • Toronto

International Standard Book Number: 0-87484-095-6

Manufactured in the United States of America

Mayfield Publishing Company
1240 Villa Street
Mountain View, CA 94041

CONTENTS

INTRODUCTION

WRITING FOR YOUR LIFE

As the authors point out in the introduction to the text, the purpose of *Motives for Writing* is to show students that authors write for different purposes; they use different modes and different strategies to fit their purpose. In teaching these strategies, the authors frequently draw upon the elements of Kenneth Burke's pentad: purpose, act, agent, agency, scene. These can be dealt with separately, or used in combinations (or ratios, in Burke's terminology), to help writers accomplish their purpose in writing.

The objective of this *Instructor's Manual* is to provide you with various strategies that can help students discern each author's purpose for writing and begin to read critically so that they understand how act, agent, agency, and scene can combine to accomplish that purpose. These teaching strategies are derived from Burke's theories that rhetoric is based on self-discovery, that knowledge emerges in the process of writing, and that the contact of minds affects the development of knowledge. In other words, students learn best when engaged in reading, writing about the pieces, and sharing their ideas within discourse communities. Reading expert Frank Smith puts it more succinctly: Learning is enhanced through demonstration, engagement, and sensitivity.

At this stage in the students' academic careers, their literacy habits are pretty well established. According to a recent educational poll, only 20 percent of sixteen- through nineteen-year-olds read books, either for pleasure or information. Thus in an average classroom of twenty-five, only five of your students are experienced readers. Early on, reading was made accessible and enjoyable to these students through demonstration. They weren't told that reading was fun; they were read to. Because of the demonstrations, these students eventually engaged in the process themselves. They read. Because of their reading experiences, either consciously or unconsciously, they became sensitive to the conventions of language—they learned how to spell and how to write a complete sentence, a developed paragraph, a narrative essay, or other discourse forms. If they have had sufficient writing experience, these five will be your best writers; if they have not written much, they will learn the easiest.

What about the other twenty? Even though they are college students (or perhaps because they are), they will read and discuss a text only when they see a purpose for doing so. They may not see school reading as enjoyable; they fully expect it to be mundane, useful only for passing tests. If they engage with the text while reading, it will be to highlight what they think will be on tests. These are not students who read closely enough to annotate a text or to be aware of its stylistic properties. They see little purpose in reading regularly, knowing full well that they won't be tested daily, that the teacher will tell them what's important, and that the "smart kids" will carry the discussion. These twenty are the students who either will not read their assignment or, at best, will skim it.

Needless to say, it's very difficult to change their attitudes. We can begin, however, by changing students' behavior and misperceptions through demonstration and engagement. Eventually, through practice, they may become sensitive to the conventions of language. The first step is to show them *how* to get involved by introducing journals and freewriting. Then we get them involved by designing and assigning journals and freewriting.

Why journals? A good journal assignment will encourage students to read and will involve them with the text by focusing their attention. Let's take the first essay in Chapter 1, "Death Valley." While the title may be promising, the topic may not be. A prereading journal assignment asking students to describe "a hard place to love" may pique their interest, but more importantly, it asks for their input, their interpretation, their descriptions. It makes them a part of the literary event. The second essay in that chapter, "Finishing School," may be more interesting to them, but students can get more involved if it is preceded by a journal entry asking them to tell about a time when they were mistreated because of another person's prejudice or ignorance about them. This type of assignment helps students relate to what's going on in the essay.

Of course, prereading journal entries are still no guarantee that students will actually go on to read. They also need postreading assignments that allow for analysis and personal response. David Groff's "Taking the Test," which recounts his reasons for and apprehensions about being tested for AIDS, ends without giving the results. A journal assignment that asks students to finish the essay from the author's point of view, describing the feelings of testing positive or negative and how this would affect their lives, not only gets them interested in reading but asks them to read in such a way that their conclusion fits the tone and style of the rest of the essay. In the process, they are again allowed to be a part of the literature.

You can also use personal response to move students into analytical reading. In Chapter 2, Annie Dillard's "Death of a Moth" may possibly be described as "weird" by the majority of your students. Fine. You can anticipate this response by giving a journal assignment in which you tell them that you think it's weird and ask them to tell what they think of it and explain *why* they feel that way. The "weird" description gives them a focus; as they read, they'll note examples or images that support it. Or they may perversely read to find reasons to disagree with you. In either instance, you have accomplished your purpose: They are reading, reading closely, and writing about what they have found.

These are just a sampling of journal entries. In this manual the notes on the readings contain at least one assignment per reading. (These should not be confused with the Suggestions for Writing that appear at the end of each reading. They were designed as essay assignments.) The majority of the assignments suggested in the notes are best written in journal form, out of class, so that students have time to read, reflect, and write—and so they will, in fact, do all three! What do you do with these suggested assignments? How do you reward the students for actually taking the time to read and then write? The important thing is to give them feedback and praise. I'm sure we'd all like to believe that the benefits and insights gained from engaging in this process should be reward enough; after all, these are college students. But that's just not the case. We all need some praise, no matter what our age, and students need it even more. We are asking them to learn a new way of reading and writing, to put more time into a class than they do ordinarily; they need some feedback. Without it, they may not do the work.

If you want to ensure that the journal work is done each day, have students hand it in at the end of each period. If you wish to give them more latitude, have them hand in all of their journals at the end of each chapter. All of this paperwork does not necessarily mean extra work for you. The students need some feedback, some tangible acknowledgment or reward for their efforts, but they don't need grades or criticism. Make it easy on yourself and beneficial for them. Since there are usually seven essays per section, each entry could be worth a seventh of 100 points—14 points for a full page, 7 points for a half, and so on. The full-page/half-page criteria makes it easy for you to respond. You can hand out the numbers based on page length and skim the journals, writing "Good idea!" where appropriate; or you can spot-check occasional entries, reading closely if you're looking for specific information that could be developed into the next full paper.

Just as students need a purpose for reading, they also need a purpose for writing these journal entries. They have to be more than busywork or thinly disguised quizzes. Another reason and application for journal entries is as a beginning point for class discussion. In *Rhetoric and Reality*, James Berlin notes that modern rhetoric carries on the spirit of Kenneth Burke through its focus on communication, contemplation, inquiry, self-expression, cooperation, mutuality, and social harmony. Meaning emerges, he says, "from individuals engaging in rhetorical discourse in discourse communities" (165–66). The students' journal entries and in-class freewritings can provide a focus for discussion within large and small discourse communities.

Collaborative Work

In the past decade, educators have increasingly recognized the value of collaborative learning and small-group discussions within the writing classroom. These smaller contexts for exchanging information seem much more conducive to discussion than the apparent threat posed by the idea of responding to the class at large. Just as there are usually five readers and twenty nonreaders per classroom, there is approximately the same ratio of students willing to respond and listen, respectively. The twenty passive ones will become much more involved in the learning process with a journal entry in front of them to be shared with or read to a small group of four to five other students. In this context, the quiet, introverted, or reluctant students seem to come alive. In the process, they learn.

While many teachers now agree that group work is a good idea, they may avoid it either because they have had no experience with it or because the experience was bad. The notes in the *Instructor's Manual* will help you. In addition to offering suggested journal entries and/or freewriting topics, they include activities to aid learning through group work and class discussion. For example, following a discussion of Ellen Goodman's "In the Male Direction" in Chapter 3, students can brainstorm examples in response to Goodman's statement that "the differences between the sexes has led to all sorts of misunderstandings and midnight hysterics." From this list, they can choose one experience for freewriting. When the freewriting is done, you can group students according to similar topics and have them develop scenes by using Goodman's techniques or one of the comedic strategies of the other writers in that chapter. Group work lets students try out ideas on each other, some of which they may have missed in their reading. At the same time, collaboration clarifies the amount of work it takes to write an effective scene yet makes it easier to try.

In addition to developing writing assignments, students can work together in groups to analyze or argue about what they have read. If you assign Martin Luther King's "I Have a Dream" and George Orwell's "A Hanging" together (Chapter 4), following some preliminary freewriting, you can divide students into groups of three to four and have them compare and contrast the two essays. This type of activity lets students learn inductively; they construct their own knowledge. Similarly, in Chapter 6, you can help students assimilate the research strategies used to develop "Peter Jennings Gets No Self-Respect" by having them brainstorm a list of people they'd like to interview; then they can work in groups developing interview questions, sharing sources, and practicing interviews on each other before actually conducting their own. One final example. In Chapter 10, after reading *Trifles,* the class can take sides on whether or not Mrs. Wright is guilty, form groups based on their beliefs, search for details within the play that support their argument, and then debate the issue. In the process, they increase their comprehension of the play, become aware of the use and value of details, and assimilate the structure of argument and counterargument.

Despite specific tasks, there may be times when group work seems chaotic and counterproductive or the bulk of the work still falls on the responsible few. Diana George's "Working with Peer Groups in the Composition Classroom" addresses many of these problems and offers possible solutions. Although her focus is on using peer groups in workshops to critique papers, her suggestions apply to all sorts of collaborative activities. George notes that there are three group "types"—task-oriented, leaderless, and dysfunctional. Their names are self-explanatory. The task-oriented group is made up of the best students (maybe those same five who read). They assign tasks, follow directions, and do a thorough job. The leaderless group has difficulty starting tasks or discussing them. Because of their hesitance, they may become dominated by the opinionated student who knows it all. She not only directs traffic but also criticizes or ignores any idea that isn't her own. The dysfunctional group may, unfortunately, be the most familiar. These students perform their tasks either listlessly or perfunctorily, finishing in ten minutes what takes the task-oriented group an entire fifty-minute period; or else they never get started because they can't even sit in a complete circle.

Through hours of observing and tape-recording group activities, George has come up with eight solutions to the less successful groups:

1. Model group discussion by using sample papers.

2. Have students bring questions about their papers to the group.

3. Have the author begin discussion with a specific question.

4. Have each writer describe her paper and the parts she's having trouble with.

5. Tape group discussions and respond to them.

6. Teach students to review their discussions at the end of each session, so the writer can take notes.

7. Meet with each group individually two to three times per semester to give feedback on their work.

8. Circulate during discussions to keep groups focused on the task.

George summarizes the teacher's task as follows: "Constantly listen, constantly watch, constantly suggest" (324–26).

Once you have the groups functioning, you may want to consider how to reward them for their work. Should you give them individual or group grades? The easiest solution is to make the end result of each group session a written document or report to turn in. In a class of twenty-five, for example, you'll receive five or six one-page reports. These can be graded like the journal entries, on a 1-to-10 scale or on a scale using a fraction of the number of days in the unit. For ease in computing, the 1-to-10 scale is probably most practical. If you use it for group work and journal entries, you needn't distinguish between the two when adding points; every ten assignments equals one letter grade. For assignment of a group grade, if group A scores a 10, then everyone in the group gets a 10; if group B only gets an 8, then everyone in it gets an 8, and so on. Criteria for awarding points should be simple: 10 points for a complete page of work, such as a scene based on Goodman or a list of interview questions based on Kaye; or 10 points per page (on a two-page limit) for comparing and contrasting King and Orwell or for listing arguments and counterarguments about Mrs. Wright. Obviously, you can make this scoring as easy or complex as you wish. What's important is that the students see that this work is meaningful. If you notice, or are told, that there are some people who consistently fail to contribute, have the group members evaluate themselves.

Group work can be adapted to most of the activities in the writing classroom. Rather than have the students individually answer the questions at the end of each reading, you can assign one or two questions per group. By collaborating on their answers, students are introduced to different points of view and different ways of reading and interpreting the stories and essays. They can also collaborate to generate ideas for writing assignments.

At the end of each essay, you'll note that the authors have included two suggested writing assignments. After Gilson's article proposing that we do away with Mother's Day (Chapter 5),one assignment asks, "If you disagree with Gilson, write an argument on behalf of giving mothers the recognition that you think they deserve." If you want students to write on this topic, they can form groups and discuss reasons why this holiday should be retained, how to organize the reasons, and ways to write an introduction that would best engage a reader. Such collaboration gives the students an edge. Instead of staring at their paper or computer screen, wondering what to say and how to say it, they have solid ideas to start with, ideas generated in the group discussions. This isn't cheating; it's how people write in the real world.

Additional Writing Assignments

This manual includes Additional Writing Assignments at the end of each chapter. These assignments link similar topics both within and between chapters and ask students to use the readings both as springboards for ideas and as models for development. They are also designed to become more complex as the text progresses from narration to persuasion to analysis.

In Chapter 1, for example, the topics are gender roles, prejudice, and the environment. The topic gender roles links the essays by Angelou, Schiel, Merton, and Norman, pointing out that they all in some ways illustrate that how, when, and where we were raised affect our perception of gender roles and how we accept them. The essay assignment asks students to tell a story that shows how one or more of these factors affected them. The complexity of the writing assignments increases by chapter, so that by the time the students get to Chapter 5, they are writing arguments. The topics there are change and individual rights. After pointing out that Weisberg, Jefferson, and Gilson all write about an individual's rights (Weisberg about gays, Jefferson about Americans, and Gilson about women), the assignment asks students to consider what rights they feel strongly about and to develop a persuasive paper, drawing upon the argumentative strategies modeled within the chapter that are appropriate for their purpose and audience. Analysis, the most difficult topic for students, comes last in Chapter 10. At this point, students are given a focus for literary analysis, such as symbol, character, or poetry. They are reminded of the authors whose works exemplify these traits and are allowed to choose a poem or short story to analyze.

The work suggested in the notes in this *Instructor's Manual* will help prepare students to write these larger essays. Additional help in the form of prewriting and organizational ideas is given within each essay assignment. However, as the essays (and, presumably, the students) progress, the assignments leave more decisions to the students.

One decision you will probably not want to leave up to them is how and when to revise their essays. The journal assignments and group work will have engaged students in their reading and writing, but they will not yet have developed the degree of critical-reading experience necessary to be sensitive to changes needed in their drafts. In fact, when they enter your class, students may not yet be sensitive to the wisdom and necessity of writing multiple drafts.

If students have been working collaboratively to discuss the readings and their journal entries, they will be accustomed to group work and be ready to redirect their efforts toward their peers' writing. But they will still need help. One of the most basic methods of response is PQP—praise, question, polish—

used in the National Writing Project summer institutes. Despite the growth of the NWP, not all your students will have experienced this method, so you will need to model it, using one of your own papers, one from another class, or one from a volunteer. The students need to become aware of the necessity for specific praise and questions. Comments like "This is really good" or "This is really bad" do not help writers revise. In "Collaborative Learning and Teaching Writing," John Trimbur quotes Ken Bruffee as saying that students "should begin with description and proceed only gradually to evaluative" responses (403). Only as they become more experienced readers can students move into more constructively critical or analytical comments.

You can guide and help develop the students' critical reading skills by developing what I call "edit sheets," lists of open-ended questions that ask for descriptive responses. If the sheets and workshops progress from a focus on content, to organization and style, and then to mechanics, students will eventually see that following this pattern enables them to fully develop their ideas before they stop their train of thought to look at mechanics. Questions on the first draft can ask: What is the best part of the paper? What makes it good? What is the purpose of this essay? What parts (if any) make you stumble? What would you like to know more about?

Questions on the second draft can reinforce the need for close reading while shifting the focus to structural elements by asking: What changes did the author make between the first and second drafts? How does the introduction engage the reader? If it doesn't, what type of introductory material would? How is the paper organized? Are there any parts that seem to be out of order? Where would you put them? How does the paper end—smoothly or abruptly? If it ends abruptly, what else does it need to do? With the third draft, the questions can focus on style and mechanics, asking students to circle misspelled or suspicious-looking words, to put a slash (/) between run-on sentences, to put question marks next to tense shifts, and so on.

You will need to help students become sensitive readers by modeling the behavior you expect. Before each workshop session, have the class spend some time on examples (taken from their previous drafts) of the type of problems that need work. They can design engaging introductions, develop flat paragraphs, tighten awkward or wordy sentences. All of this practice, immediately preceding the workshop session, should sharpen their critical-reading skills.

Of course, these are not the only ways to involve students in group work. The Bibliography at the end of this manual lists additional sources for teaching strategies and information on the issues and authors referred to here and in the students' text. I hope you find them useful.

CHAPTER 1

WRITING TO RECORD A MEMORY

The main focus in this chapter is on narrative, descriptive writing that can best be developed from observations and freewriting of journal entries. Peter Elbow's "Freewriting" is possibly the best and most specific explanation of this form of writing. Elbow explains that the idea behind freewriting

> is simply to write. . . . Don't stop for anything. Go quickly without rushing. Never stop to look back, to cross something out, to wonder how to spell something, to wonder what word or thought to use, or to think about what you are doing. If you can't think of a word or a spelling, just use a squiggle or else write, "I can't think of it." Just put down something. The easiest thing is just to put down whatever is in your mind.

(Full reference to Elbow's article, as well as to others mentioned in the text, can be found in the Bibliography at the end of this manual.) Rather than telling students what this means, show them. Try freewriting about yourself or about a memory. Hand out your freewriting to the students and have them identify what distinguishes it from traditional "school" writing.

Once students understand what freewriting is, you can have them apply it to a number of different types of journal entries. In "Journal Writing across the Curriculum," Toby Fulwiler offers the following suggestions:

1. Start class by giving students five minutes to write a journal entry. You can focus the topic (and the students' thinking) by having them respond to a quotation from the day's reading.

2. Precede the discussion of this chapter with a journal entry about memories—for instance, "Write about your memories of a favorite birthday." This type of exercise lets students see the value of writing to recall information.

3. End the class period with time for a journal entry, asking students to synthesize or apply ideas discussed in class that day. For example, if discussion focused on how to develop a scene to dramatize an issue, they could describe a scene that would be useful in their papers.

4. Interrupt a lecture or discussion with time for a five-minute journal entry. If you are introducing the idea of writing about memories, have students make a list of twenty-five childhood memories.

5. Interrupt an argumentative discussion by calling time-out and having students explain their stance. This might work well with Groff's piece on AIDS testing.

6. Use the journal to solve problems. Have students write about a line or issue they do not understand.

7. Assign a journal entry as homework. If class discussion focused on the use of an item (such as Levi's) as a symbol, the homework assignment could be to write about an item that symbolized a change in their lives.

8. Use the journal to record observations. Ask students to observe scenes to practice recording specific details. Have them all go to the same place; then they can compare their differing accounts.

9. Prior to beginning a paper on memories, have students reread all of their journal entries for this chapter and evaluate them, determining which have the greatest potential for development or were the most influential, or looking for patterns in their entries that may help them see where their interests lie.

In "Journals: Write More—Grade Less," Jane Zeni offers some specific applications for journal entries so that students can turn them into papers. To teach descriptive strategies, she suggests the following exercises: In class, have the students "develop a feel for concrete detail through exercises in close observation of interesting objects." Or have them close their eyes and picture themselves as a young child, focusing on a single scene. Then, with eyes open, have them write about how they felt at that time. To generate ideas, have them draw a "lifeline," listing major events in their lives. They can choose a writing topic from this list.

Outside class, have them use their journals to record sense impressions— sights, sounds, touch sensations, tastes, smells. To teach chronology, have them write about their day, but with a focus on "sense impressions and moods" (10). Each day, have students write about one childhood memory. After two or three weeks, have them choose the best memory to develop.

All of these journal entries can be adapted to fit the motive and mode for writing. Additional assignments are included in this manual within the notes for each essay and in the Additional Writing Assignments at the end of the notes for each chapter.

Edward Abbey, "Death Valley"

The wealth of detail and description may make this piece a little hard for some students to read and understand. You can prepare them for the reading by having them freewrite or brainstorm impressions evoked by Abbey's phrase "A hard place to love." The progression of description by season and varying location should help students note some distinctions within this excerpt. In fact, mapping is one way to help them plot the changes in scene. They can make further distinctions by incorporating into their map the various agents (e.g., animal, insect, vegetable, season, time of day, etc.) or actions that influence the changing scenery and impressions. Mapping will demonstrate the author's organizational and descriptive strategies; these in turn provide excellent models for developing a descriptive essay.

Maya Angelou, "Finishing School"

This piece is a study in contrasts. On one level, it alludes to the cultural diversity in preparing children for their adult roles; on another level, it demonstrates the similar social expectations for development of gender roles, expectations that cross racial and sociocultural lines. On a much larger level, it reveals not only the prejudices whites had for blacks but also some misperceptions blacks had about whites. A prereading assignment for this text is to have students freewrite about a time when they were mistreated because of another person's prejudice or ignorance about them. Class discussion may center on the importance of names; students can freewrite on who they were named after and why, what their name means to them, and how they would react to being "called out of their name." Discussion can also center on the reading's purpose, the author's strategies for achieving it, and the effect this piece would have on different audiences—of different races, in different times, or in different parts of the country.

Marilyn Schiel, "Levi's"

This piece is a good companion to Angelou's. Both present a view of the world from a young girl's perspective; both deal with social/gender roles; both illustrate an individual's and society's changing, or changed, attitudes; both focus, in a sense, on what are now called minority issues; in both, change is represented by a particular symbol. Class discussion can evolve out of small-group work in which each group is assigned one of these topics and is asked to compare its treatment in the two stories. While both selections are dated in terms of the changes they describe, they should provide springboards for further discussion of prejudices, changes, and the symbols representing them in the 1990s.

Andrew Merton, "When Father Doesn't Know Best"

This reading works nicely with an emphasis on gender, societal, and role expectations. It can be paired with the Schiel piece (if the Angelou/Schiel pairing didn't appeal), so that males and females can both speak about the roles and expectations of their own genders. Discussion can also focus on the changes mentioned above. While fathers have always had the role of taking their boys to the ball game, Merton seems to exemplify the modern, thoughtful, Alan Alda type of 1990s dad, quite unlike the partner to Schiel's June Cleaver mother. At the same time, however, there seem to be fewer fathers around—divorce has caused some mothers to assume the role of attending ball games with their children. Could this piece therefore have a *purpose* different from the author's intention? What *agents* have caused these changes in roles and relationships? How do the students feel about these changes?

Geoffrey Norman, "Gators"

While this reading could be paired with Merton for further discussion of family and changing gender roles, it also moves beyond these themes into a low-key critique of social and environmental issues. Since that intention may not be entirely clear, you may wish to ask students to freewrite on the author's purpose and how well it was accomplished. This type of assignment should involve all the students and demonstrate the variety of interpretations a single piece can have. If you were moving into a discussion of style, students could compare its narrative/retrospective introduction with Merton's to discuss the role of introductions in engaging them as readers and establishing the essays' context, tone, and scene.

David Groff, "Taking the Test"

This piece will provoke some interesting discussion, once you get students to overcome their initial reluctance to talk. Many students are extremely homophobic and fail to recognize that they have stereotyped homosexuals. You may want to initiate a discussion of this issue, pointing out that since approximately 10 percent of the population is gay, they probably know at least a dozen gay people without, perhaps, realizing it. This percentage suggests that at least one of your students is homosexual and is probably worrying about the direction the discussion will take. So a productive class needs to tread a fine line between no discussion at all and heated arguments leading to hostility.

One way to engage the students is to relate the topic to themselves or a loved one. A freewriting assignment answering the question "What would you do if you or a loved one had AIDS?" may make the subject easier for them to understand or deal with. Or you can use a reader response strategy and ask students to rewrite the end of the story from the author's point of view, beginning after "The door opened and my doctor's face appeared, sweaty at the end of the workday, as bemused as usual." This assignment enables students to see the author's point of view, whether or not they want to. This assignment or one similar to it will probably be necessary to get the discussion on the right track, even if you wish to focus primarily on the essay's structure and rhetorical strategies. At that point, students may want to discuss the effect of the straightforward introduction, the building suspense of the narrative, and their feelings at not being told the results. All of this will lead into a better understanding of the author's purpose in writing the piece, and ending it, as he did.

Primo Levi, "The Last Christmas of the War"

Upon a first reading, this piece may seem completely removed from the others in this chapter in terms of theme and setting. Yet the author's purpose parallels the others: He writes to recall a time, to paint a picture, to evoke feelings, to make a statement about the human condition. To make this point clearer, you may need to provide some background information on the war and Hitler's treatment of the Jews, noting that Levi was Jewish, before having students read. Then when they come to class, ask them to freewrite or brainstorm on who the author's intended audience is, which should lead them to discern his

purpose. That discovery can lead to a discussion of how he accomplishes it—
what rhetorical strategies he uses, and how they parallel those used in the other
readings in this chapter. The fact that this essay uses a memory to make a
point—employing symbol, narrative, and description; incorporating scene, acts,
agents, and agency to fulfill his purpose; building upon a particular theme and
directing it to a particular audience—makes it in many ways similar to the
others. By discussing these strategies, students should have a clearer idea of
how—and, more importantly, why—you write to record a memory.

ADDITIONAL WRITING ASSIGNMENTS

1. *Gender roles*. The readings by Angelou, Schiel, Merton, and Norman in
   some ways illustrate that how, when, and where we were raised affects our
   perception of gender roles and how we accept them. How did these factors
   affect you?

   To prepare for this assignment, think about your formative childhood
   years and the various factors that "formed" you. Here are some questions to
   consider in deciding upon a focus: What was your relationship with your
   parents? Which parent were you closer to? Who influenced you the most?
   In what ways did this parent influence you? How did your environment
   influence you? Did you live in one place (house or apartment; city or town)
   your whole life? Did you move a lot? Was a particular move influential?
   How did the decade of your youth influence your ideas about who you are
   and how you want to act?

   Once you have decided upon a focus (parent, setting, era), make a list of
   all the ideas or stories you could write about. From this list, pick two topics
   to freewrite on for five to ten minutes each. When you have finished
   freewriting, decide which topic has the most potential. Then begin drafting
   your essay. Try to incorporate some of the rhetorical strategies discussed
   and illustrated in this chapter (retrospective introductions, use of humor,
   symbols, building suspense, etc.).

2. *Prejudice*. The essays by Angelou, Schiel, Groff, and Levi illustrate different
   forms, or effects, of prejudice. While prejudice can take many forms, in
   these pieces it is based on race, gender, gender preference, or religion.
   Have you ever been a victim of prejudice? What was it based on? When did
   it happen? What forms did it take? Is there any one item or incident that
   symbolized this prejudice? How did you react to, or deal with, this
   treatment? How do you feel about the situation now? Once you have
   decided upon a memory to develop and have roughed out a draft, try to
   incorporate some of the rhetorical strategies shown in this chapter.

3. *The environment*. Abbey and Norman tell about their memories of a place.
   Their purpose seems to be to elicit appreciation for nature's wonders and
   regret for their apparent decline, respectively. While Abbey uses the
   rhetorical strategy of journal entries as a framing device, Norman presents
   his thesis by comparing past memories with the present situation.

   Think about a place you'd like to describe. What would be your motive
   for writing about this place? Using this motive, write about your memories

of this special place. In developing your essay, you can focus on a specific incident that best illustrates its significance, compare how it was with how it is now, or give an account of how and why it has changed over time.

ANSWERS TO QUESTIONS

Abbey, "Death Valley"

1. The author seems to love this place because it fascinates him; he is amazed at the variety and abundance of life in such a barren place.

2. One implication of describing humans as "other mammals" is that their survival strategies are very similar, "by burrowing deep or by constructing an artificial environment." Bugs are described as tourists because they "have learned to make a good thing off passing trade"—the smashed bugs that arrive on the human tourists' vehicles. Abbey is also making a negative comment about tourists who invade his space.

3. In Las Vegas, people survive primarily in the artificial environments of the casinos, insulated from the heat. That the economy feeds on people's greed and cupidity makes the community sterile culturally and intellectually.

4. Other metaphors use, perversely or ironically, water imagery—describing the desert as a sea "not of brine, but of heat, of shimmering simmering waves of light. . . . the sea of sand"; comparing the gravel formations to the "fabled seas of the moon" or "a lake of heat."

5. By using a journal format, Abbey can focus purely on description. He can also use it as a framing device, so that observations can proceed from season to season and/or from site to site. The advantage of this method is that it eliminates the necessity for transitions and related actions or actors; he need only focus on the view. A disadvantage is that this organizational strategy may not be immediately clear to student readers, who need these elements.

Angelou, "Finishing School"

1. Mrs. Cullinan shortens Margaret's name because she thinks it's too long to pronounce. This act goes beyond pronunciation to the white woman's attitude toward blacks: that they are subhuman, like pets, and therefore have no feelings for or rights to their given names. That Angelou eventually changed her name is probably unrelated to Mrs. Cullinan's behavior; she did so because she has that right.

2. Blacks had their own drinking glasses for the same reason that they were assigned their own drinking fountains and bathrooms—the whites didn't want to be "contaminated." They wanted to retain the idea that the races were separate and that blacks were inferior.

3. When white girls went to finishing school, they learned how to function in society. Black women learned their function in society by serving in the white women's kitchens—they learned that a woman's place is to serve and to make the home comfortable for the males.

4. Miss Glory symbolizes the traditional roles of blacks in the south; she is a female "Uncle Tom." To keep her job, she sides with her mistress. She differs from Angelou within the story in that she was raised that way and probably fears the change; she differs from her in general because Angelou represents the new generation of blacks who worked for equality.

5. Omitting the paragraph takes away a phrase that shows the extent of Angelou's anger and the clues that she will eventually quit this job. It also diminishes our sense of Angelou's voice.

Schiel, "Levi's"

1. Schiel characterizes her mother as "June Cleaver," both in dress and actions. Her mother changes because she goes to work and gets out of the house. Suddenly, those household chores don't seem so all-consuming or important; there are better, more substantive things to do. Schiel approves because it gives her mother more freedom and individuality.

2. Jeans represent freedom from the restraints traditionally placed on females in the society Schiel grew up in. The comparison of her brother's activities with her own shows how differently boys and girls were treated; the contrast between jeans and "embroidered bunnies," between sturdy pants with real pockets and easily torn slacks with inadequate pockets, shows the different expectations and treatment.

3. Paragraph 1 suggests that Schiel didn't want anything excessive or out of the ordinary; at the same time, the description sets up a series of contrasts between male and female worlds that continues throughout the essay with the repetition of "they weren't, they weren't, they weren't." Other repetitions maintain the dichotomy. Throughout the essay, Schiel compares and contrasts the two views of the sexes and their differing roles.

4. The amount of detail clearly demonstrates the amount of work expected by women.

5. Schiel's closing description of her outfit suggests that despite the gains made by her mother and other working women, the influences of peers and society were still strong, especially on young girls not immersed in the demands of the working world. It also shows that life does not require either/or choices for clothing or any other decisions. Schiel would not be enjoying freedom if she had to stick to a single new costume that had replaced the old.

Merton, "When Father Doesn't Know Best"

1. Merton's introduction sets up the tradition of men's sometimes unrealistic expectations for their sons. By using boxing as his example, he shows how extreme and potentially damaging such expectations can be.

2. Merton gets angry because his son isn't living up to his own expectations and is therefore ruining his day. He is able to salvage the day when he realizes how self-centered these expectations are.

3. Gabe seems like a typical four-year-old, quickly and easily bored, especially in a TV-dominated culture where everything changes quickly. He is shown to have some personality when Merton describes his son's apprehension at his father's anger, but both behaviors are typical behavior for a child that age.

4. The second-to-last paragraph simultaneously shows some insight on the author's part and also suggests that he hasn't given up all his expectations.

5. All of the memories are interrelated, for they show why Merton set up his expectations and how he gained some insight into their inappropriateness. All pertain to father-son relationships and how they do or do not work. They are related to *memory* in general because our memories are stored hierarchically, with large, general notions (such as "baseball games with Dad") subsuming other, more specific ones. One memory leads to another because they are all connected by certain key elements—Dad, baseball, sons, ages, and so forth.

Norman, "Gators"

1. Norman says that alligators represented "the other"—primitive, primeval creatures from another time.

2. The road kills, like the threatened alligators, are a result of society's encroachment on and disregard for the environment.

3. Marshmallows are "fake food," the nutritionless junk food representative of today's culture. Feeding this type of food to an alligator removes it from its original, natural environment and puts it on the path toward extinction. Fighting with another alligator, however, is natural—something gators have always done, regardless of the presence or absence of society.

4. Paragraphs 11 and 12 drive home the point the author tries to make through narration in the first half of the essay. They also provide a bridge to the last part of the essay. It too is a narrative, but the background paragraphs illustrate its purpose.

5. I suppose alligators are admirable because they illustrate Darwin's theory— survival of the fittest. While other creatures have become extinct, the alligator lives on. They could be considered important because they represent our past, a time when humans weren't killing off everything

because of a total disregard for the importance of the environment. They also are strong and know who they are.

Groff, "Taking the Test"

1. Groff's candor in declaring his sexual preference in print seems to parallel gays' reasons for "coming out"—they feel the need to live an honest life and to publicize and personalize the horrors of AIDS. To write without this revelation would lessen the impact of the essay: It would become a depersonalized account that readers could dismiss as unrelated to their lives. The author's honesty in this essay also helps to establish that he has genuine grounds for concern.

2. The scene suggests both fear and anger. He's afraid of what he'll learn and yet angry at the public's perception (and misperception) of the disease and of gay men in particular.

3. The woman in black subtly reminds readers that AIDS is not a disease confined to gay males or black drug abusers; anyone can get it.

4. Groff's appreciation for life changes, either because it will continue or because he has little time left to experience it.

5. The test results would probably affect the readers' perceptions of and appreciation for the drama this essay builds. By leaving the ending ambivalent, Groff suggests that anyone can get AIDS. If he had said that his tests were positive, readers might have dismissed the whole thing as being something that happens only to gay males. If the results had been negative, readers might have concluded, "Well I'm glad this story had a happy ending; now I don't have to worry about it."

Levi, "The Last Christmas of the War"

1. Paragraph 2 shows the slow progress toward the end of the war. Levi shows the type of bombing to illustrate the Allies' intent—stop the war without killing everyone or totally damaging the economy but also let the death camps keep functioning.

2. Christmas is about rebirth and the forgiveness taught to us by a child; the Hitler Youth represent children taught to hate. They pervert the idea of Christmas.

3. Frau Mayer represents the human side of the war and shows that not all Germans were evil. It was risky for Levi to speak with or work for her because it took time away from his work; he did it because he was hungry. She may have whispered about Christmas as a word of encouragement, since to Christians, Christmas is a time of hope and celebration.

4. Levi's story about the refrigeration failure suggests that people survived concentration camps through their wits. Levi had the added advantage of

being a professional, so his treatment and conditions may have been marginally better.

5. Levi's Christmas gift was special because it aided not only his physical survival, by providing much-needed food, but also his spiritual/psychological survival, by establishing or reaffirming a link with the outside world.

6. Levi has the gift of loving and friendship, as exemplified in his relationship with his friend Alberto. That they can share and forgive, even in these conditions, illustrates the meaning of Christmas.

CHAPTER 2

WRITING TO DISCOVER ONESELF

Since the readings in this chapter continue to revolve around or emerge from introspection, the students' journals will continue to be a source of ideas and (hopefully) insight. The primary topics in this chapter are parents' influences on their children's ideas and self-image; how people are defined by language; fundamental beliefs; and change, turning points, and growth in self-knowledge. You can help students generate and develop ideas about these topics by assigning daily journal entries, to be done both inside and outside class.

In class, the students can work together to generate a list of topics. To determine parental influence, have the students divide a paper in half. On one side, they will list characteristics and beliefs that define their parents or another adult important in their childhood (keep in mind that some students may have no memory of at least one of their parents). On the other side, they will list their own. Characteristics might include physical features such as height, weight, shape, hair color, nose size, skin color; typical activities like reading, playing golf, going to church, or watching TV; speech habits in public and private, such as modes of arguing, negotiating, persuading, or cajoling. Beliefs can range from religious to superstitious, from morals to mores, from work habits to theories of leisure, from gender roles to racial or sexual stereotypes. You can start the discussion by providing some examples of your own on the board. Then ask students to complete their own lists. When they have finished, compile a master list on the board so that they can see the variety of traits to choose from. From this list, they should be able to select enough characteristics to develop journal entries for a week.

Another strategy for generating ideas is to redo the lifeline developed in the previous chapter. This time, focus on influential people, activities, and events. Have students do one line, focusing on only one aspect at a time. Influential people may not immediately stand out; however, if students begin with important activities, the people involved may emerge as the events are recalled. Once these two elements are in place, students can stand back and re-mark the line to indicate major events or turning points. While each lifeline will be unique to that student's experiences, sharing major events in a class lifeline on the board is also useful, since it can jog the students' memories. There may be some incidents that do not seem important until they are seen in relation to others during the same time period. Collaborative work can help bring these events to the surface. At the same time, this type of structured activity should give students the distance they need to write with perspective.

Outside class, students can take the time they need to think about and develop their thoughts and memories. With seven selections, this chapter, like the others in the text, will probably take about two weeks to cover. If you assign a ten-minute journal entry per day, the students will have about ten to fourteen entries from this chapter to choose from, as well as those from Chapter 1, when it's time to develop their essay.

When you reach that point, some class time may be devoted to a discussion of modes. Ask the students to classify their journal entries: Which ones would make a strong narrative? What two could be paired to show a contrast or marked change in beliefs or life-style? Which person or event is the most significant? What person or issue keeps recurring? What item or action symbolizes change? You can model this activity by having students classify the essays in this chapter. If they are willing, you can have students exchange journals so that their partner or group members do a similar analysis. Their objective insights may yield groupings or classifications the writer had not recognized.

After these analyses have been concluded, you may move in one of two different directions. You can have students choose the two entries or topics with the most potential and double the length, to see which would make the best essay. Or you can ask them to read the Suggestions for Writing (at the end of each reading in the text) or give them the Additional Writing Assignments (in this manual) and let them decide which entries could be developed to fit the topic. This combination of reading, writing, and working collaboratively should yield some insightful papers.

Scott Russell Sanders, "Grub"

This piece is one of those foolers—students will probably think it is only about food, when actually the descriptive passages lead the author to ponder his own roots. Students can be easily led to see his point, however, by listing or clustering their favorite childhood foods, then freewriting to examine why they like them, where they ate them, what they remind them of, what they reveal about their pasts or personalities. Following that discussion, ask the students to point out particularly vivid, descriptive passages and discuss how Sanders uses language to make us see, smell, and taste the food. Once those passages have been established as models, ask students to choose one of their favorite foods and, using the same descriptive strategies, describe it to make it appeal to their listeners' or readers' senses.

Richard Rodriguez, "Complexion"

Although many people would consider Richard Rodriguez a handsome man, this reading reveals his concern about and dislike of his complexion. His feelings demonstrate the effect that parents and upbringing can have on one's self-image. You can find this dichotomy in the excerpt and throughout the book it's taken from, *The Hunger of Memory*. Raised poor, he wanted to be rich; made aware of his Hispanic heritage, he wanted to be white; a barrio resident, he ran around with well-to-do white kids. The result is a man who grows up feeling that he doesn't fit in; he denies his heritage, but he never forgets it.

While most students may not identify with the focus on complexion, they probably all have some physical feature that they've grown to dislike or that they feel marks or identifies them. A freewriting on this subject, and where these feelings came from, will reveal to the class not only the similarities they share but also the influences of family and culture. This could lead, in turn, to a discussion of how perception of one's background is influenced by the ideals— which very few of us can live up to—perpetuated by society.

Steve Tesich, "An Amateur Marriage"

On the surface, this piece doesn't seem to say much. There is no particular scene, there are no characters beyond the narrator, and the only action is his marriage. Yet we can identify, just as we did with Sanders and Rodriguez, a certain philosophy of life. Perhaps the reason this point isn't immediately clear is that, unlike the other two essays, this one doesn't contain much background about family or family life. Practically the only thing we know about the author is that he doesn't believe marriage requires work and that he doesn't "consider it an accomplishment of any kind" that he has remained married for thirteen years. The other difference between this essay and the others is that this one contrasts inner feelings with those expected by social convention. Pointing out this contrast may help students enter the piece, since nearly everyone has had the experience of wondering, "How come I'm not feeling the way I'm supposed to be feeling—like everyone else is?" This type of question provides a good focus for freewriting. You can also have students write about where they gained their philosophy of life and marriage.

Annie Dillard, "The Death of a Moth"

Students' first reaction to this reading will probably be "weird." That's a good place to start. Asking students why they thought this essay is weird will make them focus on specific details in the two main scenes—Dillard's carefully observing the spider's activities and counting the carcasses, and her camping alone and watching the moth burn for two hours. How are these details related to her living alone? How are they related to her profession as a writer? The students can personalize this essay by writing on what they do when they are alone—what they observe; why they observe it; how these observations reflect their personalities, intended professions, or life-styles.

Joan Didion, "On Keeping a Notebook"

Didion's refrain "It all comes back" may be a good place to start with this piece. In saying that, she refers not only to her memories but also to the fact that writing about them in her notebook helps her recall and learn from them. In an English class, freewriting is the most obvious example of what she means, although we know this happens whenever we write. Have the students freewrite about a memory—grandmother, birthdays, picnics, or the like. Writing about these topics always elicits forgotten images or details, thus illustrating your (and Didion's) point. This piece can also be linked with Rodriguez's. Both illustrate the effects of parental influence and past events on the direction one's life takes. One follow-up to this discussion is to have students discuss their attitudes toward writing—where and how were they formed? What role does writing play in their lives?

Linda Bird Francke, "The Ambivalence of Abortion"

This reading may be as difficult to discuss as Groff's "Taking the Test." If you want to give both genders equal time, you can assign the two essays together. Like the Groff essay, this one may engender stereotypical views difficult (for you) to deal with objectively. So again, personalizing the essay may be one way to avoid the usual prejudices. You can ask students to write about how they would feel if their mother were to become pregnant and chose to have an abortion. The responses should lead them to an understanding of the complexity of the issue as well as a definition of *ambivalence* in this context. Once that definition is established, students can better analyze the reading to determine if, indeed, any ambivalence is present. What rhetorical or linguistic cues suggest that the author is anything but ambivalent?

Barbara Mellix, "From Outside, In"

Most students, whether black or white, should be able to relate in some ways to this essay. No matter what their high school training, the majority must learn the "language of the academy" when they begin college classes. If this is a freshman composition class, they may not have yet had much writing experience in their other courses. But they probably have some doubts or worries. A freewriting assignment asking them to describe similar writing experiences, or fears about them, should help them identify with Mellix's message. Her final sentence, "I write and continually give birth to myself," is a good statement to respond to and elicit discussion, either in this context or in relation to Didion's piece. This essay also works well in conjunction with Rodriguez's in terms of parents' influences on their children's self-image and subsequent success.

ADDITIONAL WRITING ASSIGNMENTS

1. *Life-styles.* The essays by Sanders, Rodriguez, and Dillard all touch on or discuss different life-styles and their influences. Sanders looks at rural living and its effects on eating habits; Rodriguez discusses poverty in the barrio and how his parents' hard lives and heritage affected him; Dillard's essay shows the effects of living alone. How does your life-style reflect your early upbringing, or how did your childhood influence who you are and how you live?

2. *Parents.* Rodriguez, Didion, and Mellix frame their essays with vignettes describing their parents. Rodriguez's mother made him aware of his skin color; Didion's mother told her to be quiet and write; Mellix's parents made sure their children spoke well. None of these memories are unusual; we all characterize our parents by particular things they said to us. Make a list of sayings or warnings your parents tended to repeat to you and/or to your

siblings. Decide which one was most influential; then consider ways to show this influence and its effects. Rodriguez and Mellix used a number of quotations from their parents; Didion used just one from them but numerous examples from her journals. Write an essay that shows your parents' influence on the person you are today.

3. *Experience.* Tesich thinks you don't need to work at marriage; Francke thinks she's ambivalent about abortion; Didion and Mellix believe that writing can change your life. Tesich, Francke, Didion, and Mellix all reflect upon how we change because of what we do. How have your experiences affected your views? If you make a list of important experiences, you may begin to see how they have affected your life and the way you view it. Choose one or two memorable experiences to freewrite about; then select the one that had the most impact and tell the reader about it. Your purpose in writing is to show how experience changes people.

ANSWERS TO QUESTIONS

Sanders, "Grub"

1. Sanders eats out when he's "on the road or feeling sorry for" himself. On this day, he's alone for the weekend and has a flooded basement and a malfunctioning car. He has chosen Ladyman's because of its atmosphere, "tacky in a timeless way."

2. Sanders is getting older, his metabolism is slowing down, and he has become aware of the dangers of high cholesterol. Consequently, he watches what he eats.

3. The first paragraph sets up a straw man: the state of Indiana, home of the fat. This setting explains what follows—overweight people eating fattening foods. Once that scene is established, Sanders can add additional details without detracting from the tone.

4. The waitress punctuates the action with her questions and urgings to "eat up." Her behavior imitates the grandmother Sanders recalls, as she saves him from his awful omelet with offerings of fresh biscuits.

5. If readers didn't pay attention to Sanders's waist size (32 before breakfast, 33 after), they might be led to think he was another Indiana fatty because of his obvious love of food. The woman reading *Cosmopolitan* may not realize that she is one of the two thin persons in the restaurant or that she may one day end up like the overweight customers.

Rodriguez, "Complexion"

1. Rodriguez sees himself as less attractive than the rest of his family because of his dark complexion and "Indian" appearance. His broodings on his complexion suggest he would prefer lighter skin.

2. The women in Rodriguez's family seemed preoccupied by skin color, especially when their children were light-skinned, and they exchanged recipes for lightening the skin of their dark ones. The men also commented on it, although their views were couched in affectionate pet names such as *mi negra* (my black one). All his relatives, despite their respect for light skin, also used that as a focus of derision about Anglos.

3. Wearing a uniform or doing manual labor is clearly associated with lower-class, menial activities and servitude.

4. Going to the opera represented the promise of the good life, the life of luxury. When it was clear that he could never attain that standard of living, Rodriguez's father quit going. In essence, he gave up his dream.

5. When Rodriguez calls himself his "parents' child," he realizes that he also feels like an outsider, the "dark little boy" who will never fit into the white world. Like his parents, he is also very class-conscious and polite.

Tesich, "An Amateur Marriage"

1. Tesich begins by talking about birthdays because he always expected he would change when he reached the most important one—age sixteen. The fact that he didn't then, or at later milestones, sets the scene for his discussion of marriage and how it hasn't changed him either.

2. Tesich's self-description suggests that he had not grown up by the time he married and that different situations elicited differing levels of (im)maturity.

3. Tesich thinks marriage reduces to whether or not you like your partner, whether you can stand to be with each other alone. He maintains that those feelings can't be worked on or developed.

4. After stating that no milestones have ever changed him, Tesich ends by discovering that he has indeed changed. Both he and his wife have grown together, and in the process, their marriage (which he refers to as "climate") has improved. He likes being married.

Dillard, "The Death of a Moth"

1. Dillard's description of and focus on her living arrangements are related to the story—if she didn't live alone or if she had someone to talk to and joke with, she wouldn't have gone camping by herself and probably would not have noticed the burning moth.

2. Dillard jokes with her cat because that is who she sleeps with. And since the story is about being alone and having only a cat to joke with, the cat becomes the surrogate spouse or lover—the usual object of such a question.

3. She went camping alone because she has no steady companion and she wants to renew her desire to write. Her reading is not light fiction; it's a serious biography, well written. The fact that she first read it when she was sixteen suggests that she has always been a serious person, dedicated to the arts. That she's reading it "hoping it would do it [make her want to be a writer] again" hints that she may be tiring of her profession or running dry.

4. The angels' wings could symbolize a feeling of redemption, rebirth, or rejuvenation, which is why Dillard went camping. Earlier in the story, Dillard compares the pile of moth carcasses to a "jumble of buttresses for cathedral vaults"; following the angels' wings passage, Dillard compares the burning moth to "an immolating monk" and, later, to a "hollow saint, like a flame-faced virgin gone to God."

5. By viewing the moth as a female, Dillard can relate to its female martyrdom and personify it as a virgin, something pure. Male personifications don't usually lend themselves to these associations.

6. After staring at a burning moth for two hours, and daily examining their dead bodies on her bathroom floor, Dillard probably knows a great deal about "what moths look like, in any state." An in-depth knowledge of a moth's body probably doesn't seem important; however, for a writer, increasing one's powers of observations is always useful.

Didion, "On Keeping a Notebook"

1. Didion seems to raise questions to anticipate a reader's objections and to serve as a springboard to examine her own motives. She uses this technique in paragraphs 5, 12, 13, 14, and 17 to question her recording of certain details and then to explain their presence and value.

2. Didion isn't interested in keeping a diary, because a dairy means keeping records and dealing with reality. Instead, she records details and impressions to use in her writing, as sources for introspection.

3. She doesn't readily admit why she keeps a journal, because it is full of details important only to herself—and she was raised to believe "that others, any others, all others, are by definition more interesting than ourselves." So keeping a journal seems egocentric and selfish.

4. Didion learns that Fitzgerald's maxim is true: The rich are different from you and me. In this case, the Greek shipping heiress is totally removed from reality.

5. Mrs. Brooks represents the old, moneyed, cultured leisure class; Mrs. Fox represents the *nouveau riche* who lack culture and taste. The distinction helps Didion remember how things (and people) used to be.

6. Didion presents herself as a careful observer; her observations reveal her as having an inquiring mind and as being sensitive to others, a little disdainful of the thoughtless rich, careful about her own thoughts and motives, and wistful for the culture of days gone by.

Francke, "The Ambivalence of Abortion"

1. A bar is a fairly impersonal place to exchange news of such import. It suggests the need not to celebrate (as with her previous pregnancies) but to drink and cushion the brain for a discussion of "bad news." Lexington Avenue is in the middle of New York City, also an impersonal place representative of the society we live in now. It's a much different setting from, say, a cozy corner tavern. Her husband's stirring fills the relative silence between them and shows his nervousness.

2. The timing wasn't right for their careers, and their children had both reached school age. For these reasons, Francke believed that she was having an abortion only because another child would be an inconvenience.

3. The repetition shows, succinctly, how the conversation went on and on and around in circles. They agreed that abortion was the right decision, but they weren't comfortable with it.

4. Francke is ironic when she notes "how very considerate they are at the Women's Services" in scheduling her promptly. Later, when she's feeling the pain of the abortion, she states, "What good sports we women are. And how obedient," as she lets the abortion proceed.

5. The children's attention is deflected because the parents don't want to go into any explanation of why Francke is bedridden; the children wouldn't understand and don't need to know.

6. The effectiveness of the ghost scene probably depends upon one's views about abortion. It can be seen as grossly and inappropriately sentimental or as a moving indictment against a society that permits abortions to continue.

Mellix, "From Outside, In"

1. *Standard English* is the term used to describe language use appropriate to and necessary for success in the professional world—a knowledge of the conventions. *Proper English* is a term more likely used to denigrate those we feel do not speak as they should—like us.

2. Within the context of her family, Mellix uses the language she was brought up with, referred to as BEV—black English vernacular—by linguists. Within

other contexts, her language shifts according to whom she speaks or writes. On the job or with whites, she would probably use standard English.

3.   Mellix feels that black English is appropriate within familiar contexts. It is not inferior; it's just another way of speaking. Because she did not grow up speaking standard English, she found it difficult to switch contexts and sound natural. To do so, she had to become comfortable with that particular vernacular, just as one best learns a foreign language by living among native speakers.

4.   On the negative side, language is equated with power because those in power speak standard English. On a more positive note, language can be equated with power because the ability to use language, to adapt it to the appropriate context and register, greatly expands a person's ability to persuade and communicate.

5.   Language has generative power because writing aids thinking. Many times, the act of writing or speaking helps people clarify their thoughts; in the act of communication, the exchange of ideas can lead to a new understanding or the development of new concepts. Writing theorists, such as Janet Emig, argue that writing (more than speaking) can "bring new selves into being" because writing can be reexamined, reread, and worked over. With every reading, we learn something new from our writing, which can lead us to further exploration.

CHAPTER 3

WRITING TO AMUSE OTHERS

This chapter is one of the distinctive features of the text. The readings provide students with a welcome change of pace, while the writing assignments ask them to write in a mode they are seldom allowed to enjoy. Although the humor in this chapter is varied, the topics and purposes for writing are related. The general topoi are human frailty, traditional standards and gender roles, and language use and abuse. But these can be expanded so that students can find a topic they know and feel strongly about. A series of heuristics—invention questions—can help them decide upon a topic and approach to writing humor.

People. Who is the funniest person you know? The most bizarre? The most naive? What makes them humorous? Who is the rudest boss/teacher/professor you ever had? What made her so rude? What kind of people make you crazy? What do they do? Who do you know that is always a victim? What happens to him? Who is the biggest neurotic you know? What does she fear? Who is the most naive or innocent person you know? What is the result of his naivete? What about yourself makes you or others crazy? What parallels are there between you and the characters you've read about in this chapter, or between you and the authors?

Animals and inanimate objects. What animals (or insects or reptiles) do you most like or dislike? What makes them appealing or disgusting? What humans do they remind you of? What kinds of machinery give you problems? Cars? Computers? Power tools? Household appliances? What situations (involving these tools), which were maddening at the time, now appear funny? How did you get your "revenge" on these objects? What situations—jobs, classes, relationships—always seem to end in disaster? What situations make you laugh? What kinds of things—weather, malls, religion, mom's cooking, sports teams or fans, TV shows or movies—are funny to you, or so irritating that they are funny?

Traditional roles and rules. What characteristic of the opposite sex makes you crazy? What elements of your own gender are ridiculous or embarrassing? What rules do you refuse to obey? How do you avoid them? What do you find humorous or annoying about the government, either local, state, or federal? How do politicians change when elected to office? What aspect about them—their attitudes, language, affectations, disregard for the people who elected them—makes you cringe? What would you change if you could?

Language use and abuse. What types of language abuse would you like to change? What are the characteristics of this usage? What type of person talks like this? Where would one find this type of language abuse? How can we stop it?

Once the students have developed a list of potential topics, they need to consider various modes of development. Some of the most common are narrative, comic portraits, social commentary, parody, and satire. In *Fact and Artifact*, Lynn Bloom explains the rationale for and components of each.

The humorous narrative is fairly straightforward—a funny story. Some examples of narratives are an account of a misadventure, a story about an initiation, or a reminiscence about a comic situation that didn't seem that funny at the time. A comic portrait may also be a narrative, but its focus is on a particular character type. Comic portraits can also be a series of vignettes— scenes that illustrate the subject's fatal—or in this case, humorous—flaws, best illustrated through exaggeration.

Humorous social commentary usually takes on social issues, such as Royko's critique of fitness fanatics. This mode is characterized by exaggerated language, satire, and often absurd comparisons; and it can take various forms—a narrative, a comic portrait, or a supposedly straightforward essay, as in Swift's "Modest Proposal." Parody can fall into this category as well; the author can use it to imitate yet ridicule known forms, such as fairy tales, detective stories, or soap operas.

Certain types of humor seem to fit certain forms. At the same time, we can also say that certain types of people tend to write certain types of humor—or feel that they are incapable of writing well, let alone writing something funny. By providing a variety of heuristics to generate ideas and forms to fit them into, you should be able to help most students develop an essay that fits their humorous bent. But if there are some who cannot, let them do the humorous analysis offered in the Additional Writing Assignments that follow the notes in this chapter.

Mike Royko, "Farewell to Fitness"

This piece should be one that many of your students can relate to, even though they are young. Not everyone was cut out to be thin, a jock, or a jogger. Students who can't relate to this reading may want to take the opposite stance, poking fun at those mid-lifers who will do anything to retain the image of youth. Whatever side they take, your students should have no trouble brainstorming fitness-related objects of derision. The hard part is to come up with details that show the humor of the situation and then weave them into an entire scenario. Some of Royko's techniques for showing humor are use of specific words (*geezer, emaciated*) and lists—of adjectives, activities, foods. He creates a cohesive scenario by providing details of the unpleasant consequences of working out. Have your students search for these techniques to use as models, choose a fitness-related "type" to poke fun at, and emulate Royko to show the humor in these situations. This task may work best if students are put into groups of two or three to share ideas and descriptions.

Woody Allen, "Spring Bulletin"

Although Woody Allen is hilarious to read, his style is hard to emulate, possibly because his brand of humor is so unique. Pointing out to students that he makes us laugh by moving from straightforward prose about commonplace situations to deadpan insertion of an absurd detail is probably not enough to enable them to model his style. If students are interested in imitating this approach, suggest that they read more. Allen's books of short stories (*Getting Even, Without Feathers, Side Effects*) provide some excellent (and classic) models. Once they analyze the characteristics of his style, students may decide that there are other comedians who have a similar approach. (Stephen Wright comes to mind.) To attune them to the techniques of humorous writing, you could bring in clips from one of Woody Allen's comic films, such as *Bananas*, or tapes of comedians doing their routines. MTV's "Half Hour Comedy Hour," showcasing a series of stand-up comedians, provides numerous examples of current approaches. For more traditional approaches, you could also bring in tapes of Burns and Allen reruns, which are regularly shown on cable.

Calvin Trillin, "Literally"

After Woody Allen, Trillin's style of humor may be hard to discern or appreciate. If students don't care for this piece, ask them why. Their dislike may be due to a generation gap. Using language as a source of humor is a fairly dry approach but a popular one with people of Trillin's generation. Once the students are aware of his technique, ask them for examples of other comedians who use this same approach (Norm Crosby, George Carlin), and the gap may become clearer. This realization probably won't make him any funnier, though. If this piece is a bomb, you can move the discussion into the purposes of his approach. What is the effect of making fun of language? Who would appreciate this type of humor? How might it empower them? Why doesn't the students' generation appreciate this approach?

Ellen Goodman, "In the Male Direction"

Differences between the sexes is always a good source of humor and is one that most students can relate to. Goodman's statement that "the differences between the sexes have led to all sorts of misunderstandings and midnight hysterics" is a good starting point: Ask students to think about situations that illustrate her statement. Then have them freewrite an experience that exemplifies one of these situations. Once they have written and shared their ideas, group them according to similar topics (if there are any). Have them develop scenes by using Goodman's techniques (citing "historical" or "scientific" evidence, assuming a position of superiority) or one of the strategies modeled by the other writers in this chapter.

Dave Barry, "A Solution to Housework"

You may want to pair this essay with Goodman's. Both point out the differences between the sexes, and both poke fun at men. Including a male author on this topic may deflect any charges of reverse sexism. Both authors also use exaggeration for humorous effect, so the modeling will be clearer and stronger. Syfers's "I Want a Wife" (from Chapter 4) continues in this vein. Obviously, you don't want to indulge in acrimonious debate here, but this grouping of essays should elicit thoughtful comments and counterarguments from the males in the class, which can be used as topics for their own humorous writing. Perhaps more importantly, this series of essays marks a good point to discuss the purpose and direction of humorous writing. Why is gender difference a more popular topic for comedians than, say, language use? Why do some women fail to see the humor in the former? How have they evened the score? What do the emergence, growing popularity, and topics of female humor say about American society and attitudes? Are they changing?

Anna Quindlen, "A Baseball Wimp"

Because of its length and focus, Quindlen's essay can be linked with Barry's on gender differences. Like Dave Barry, she pokes fun at her own sex and sideswipes the opposite. Unlike Barry's piece, however, hers might be viewed as more derogatory toward women because it makes them seem like stereotypical dimwits when it comes to sports. If you compare Quindlen's piece with Barry's, you can ask students what attitudes are conveyed and how they know this—what strategies are used? Are the stereotypes Quindlen perpetuates more dangerous, or damaging, than Barry's about men? Or can men's distaste for and women's seeming devotion to housework be equated with men's devotion to and women's ignorance of sports? The answers to these questions can form the basis of some interesting argument papers or, on the lighter side, can elicit short pieces that caricature male-female differences on other subjects.

Andy Rooney, "Old Friends"

Rooney and Royko make a good pair. Both choose a straw man to personalize complaints against a common human situation, using dialogue to make the piece more humorous and realistic. Asking students "What kinds of irritating things do your friends feel free to say to you?" should elicit a number of parallel examples. This question can also be extended to family, since they, too, will say things that no stranger ever would. Because these scenes and actors are so familiar, students should have little trouble creating a humorous paper of their own, modeling it on Rooney's. This type of writing assignment accomplishes two goals: It's manageable for practically every student, thus giving them confidence. At the same time, it painlessly teaches them how to use dialogue for comic effect.

ADDITIONAL WRITING ASSIGNMENTS

1. *Analysis.* Some people just aren't funny. They may appreciate humor, but they can't write it. If you feel that writing a comic piece is beyond you, this assignment is designed for you. In this chapter, you have seen different styles of humor that can be identified with different genders or generations. Using one of these classifications, analyze the type of humor used—topics,

approaches, or delivery—and discuss how it defines the particular society or era in which it was or has become popular. You may analyze the work of the authors in this section, as well as stand-up comedians on television or in the movies. Decide upon a type of humor—barbs aimed at male or female stereotypes; jokes about language, the environment, politics, society; self-deprecating humor—then take it apart. What makes it funny? What makes it popular? Why has it become popular, remained in vogue, or departed from the scene?

2. *Gender.* Goodman, Barry, Quindlen, and to some extent Trillin use male-female differences as a backdrop or focus for their humor. Goodman uses asking for direction, Barry uses housework, Quindlen uses sports, and Trillin uses marital misunderstandings as a focus to expound on or make fun of these differences. Obviously, each one has a purpose, a point to make. Decide on one male-female difference you find irritating or particularly ludicrous and develop a humorous essay about it. Try to use some of the comic strategies demonstrated in this chapter to develop the humor and characterization in your essay. As you draft your paper, consider your purpose and audience. Why are you writing this piece? Can you amuse without offending?

3. *Language.* Although their styles are totally opposite, both Allen and Trillin use language as a source of humor. One parodies stuffy language, while the other looks at the effect of context, but both have a purpose. If language is important to you, then its misuse or abuse by different people or in different situations may be annoying. The best way to make your point without sounding like a snob is with humor. Make a list of types of language, language abuse, or language abusers you find irritating. From this list, choose the one for which the most examples, or particular individuals, come to mind. You can generate ideas by clustering examples around that focus. This cluster may reveal related actions or scenes that will work well in an essay. From the cluster, develop an essay that makes a point by poking fun at a language abuse (or abuser).

ANSWERS TO QUESTIONS

Royko, "Farewell to Fitness"

1. Usually after "No more excuses," writers or speakers will go into a description of how they plan to change. Royko also surprises his readers when he states that the result of his obsession with handball was that he "stopped eating pork shanks," and that slower pulse levels, smaller pants, and increased time for narcissism are the only benefits. Similarly, after pointing out that exercise helps you live longer, he notes that he remembered this at his doctor's wake.

2. Royko uses exaggeration to great effect when he describes broiled skinless chicken as "the skinned flesh of a dead chicken," when he predicts that living longer will lead to euthanasia, and when he describes, in paragraph 19, how physically fit, middle-aged men behave.

3. Royko's age is significant because his message appeals to readers of the same age and thus seems to have some legitimacy. If he had been nineteen when he wrote the piece, it would be dismissed by readers, because he wouldn't have the experience to back up what he's saying.

4. Royko wants to age gracefully. Living longer can only lead to incarceration in a nursing home, surviving on Social Security.

5. Royko is making fun of people's obsessions with youth. He writes to suggest that we accept ourselves and our lives and get the most from what we have.

Allen, "Spring Bulletin"

1. Allen seems to understand that anyone who reads him will not take him seriously. Use of the term "unextended adult" is an example; it's obviously silly, both in form and image. Literally, an *extended* adult would be one who took adult education courses, or a person much taller or fatter than Woody Allen.

2. The catalog sounds familiar because Allen uses its terminology and passive-voice phrasing. He exaggerates the contents of some courses and titles of course offerings.

3. Only people familiar with the tone and language would appreciate this piece, for they would recognize it as a parody. This piece would probably reinforce the stereotyped view that higher education is useless and unrelated to the realities of society.

4. Allen likes to play with language and upset people's expectations; he also likes to poke holes in pseudointellectual postures. He isn't making fun of college education but, rather, the people who write the course descriptions.

Trillin, "Literally"

1. A *fluke* is a flatfish, as well as a stroke of luck.

2. By using a foreign word, Trillin attempts to establish himself as a learned man who knows his vocabulary. He is also presenting himself as something of a foreigner in the countryside. This persona enables him to take offense at the atrocities committed on the English language.

3. *Pump-priming, it's a fluke, make hay while the sun shines, you've got a long row to hoe, looked . . . with new eyes, getting . . . too far out on a limb, small potatoes, time and tide wait for no man, not the only fish in the sea, it's nothing but skin and bones, I have other fish to fry, slim*

pickings, everything has gone to seed, they scared the pants off me. Trillin attempts to make these clichés humorous by putting them into supposedly confusing contexts.

4.   Trillin is pointing out that we should avoid clichés.

Goodman, "In the Male Direction"

1.   Goodman's introduction establishes her as a liberal, open-minded person as well as a person of some experience. This stance should make her acceptable to readers of either sex.

2.   She sequences her examples to establish historical precedent for her father's behavior. She is also employing bathos for comic effect since a road trip with her father did not end in death.

3.   Goodman exaggerates men's unwillingness to ask for help or directions.

4.   "Men have better spatial abilities; women have better verbal abilities. . . . Men read maps and women read people. . . . The average man uses instruments. The average woman uses the voice."

5.   Goodman is relatively successful at calling humorous attention to an acknowledged gender difference. The degree of her success is probably determined by the sex of the person reading the piece and that person's experience in similar situations.

Barry, "A Solution to Housework"

1.   According to Barry, the housewives on commercials are cheerful idiots. That characterization seems pretty realistic.

2.   "Smear and shine" implies that most people would rather do a cursory, surface-level job.

3.   Barry praises women for the fact that they are willing to do housework and that they do it well. His characterization of the women in commercials also displays his recognition that housework is neither easy nor fun. All of this should appeal to female readers.

4.   Barry is drawing attention to the fact that men are shirkers when it comes to housework and do less than their share.

5.   The last sentence presents Barry as among the worst of the males rather than as a self-righteous cleaner. But Barry's intent is surely ironic. Since the essay as a whole emphasizes that cleaning is work, Barry is poking fun at himself by pretending to be a typical male.

Quindlen, "A Baseball Wimp"

1. Quindlen is called a baseball wimp because she doesn't follow the game throughout the entire season; she only gets interested toward the end. She seems to have followed the game for quite a long time and knows the basics. Her attraction to the game is probably typical of a certain segment of the population, for the same end-of-season attraction can be seen in people who only watch the basketball or football play-offs.

2. Quindlen describes her position to demonstrate the degree to which she is devoted to baseball—during the World Series. The fact that the cabdriver is Thai helps to establish the New York City setting and to suggest that baseball transcends cultural differences.

3. Quindlen's strategy is to make the joke on herself so that readers won't find her attitude irritating, as when she admits forgetting that Reggie Jackson no longer plays for New York (in fact, he no longer plays baseball) or when she says some player is cute. However, this "dumb woman" ploy might irritate feminists.

4. End-of-season baseball parallels soap operas in that both can be cliff-hangers. The allusion to the soaps is clear—"As the World Turns."

Rooney, "Old Friends"

1. The dialogue is almost entirely dependent upon the scene, since all the comments from the friends relate to the house.

2. Old friends are less hesitant to point out flaws and foibles. They know the people better, and they think they know what the people will put up with. New friends may not be so cavalier, since they want to preserve the friendship and aren't aware of potential sore spots. That is why Rooney doesn't want to invite old friends out next time.

3. Barbara and Quintin probably represent an amalgam of traits and conversations from a variety of friends. They may be pseudonyms, or given Rooney's crusty temperament, they may be real people and this is his method of revenge for their insensitive comments.

4. Rooney relies on dialogue because it is funnier, more specific, and more realistic than merely reporting the kinds of things people say. The humor depends in part upon hearing Barbara and Quintin say things that are characteristic of them.

5. Rooney is willing to drink from the jelly glass because he doesn't think it's important. He includes that detail to illustrate his attitude about picky points such as matching glasses. Unlike his guests, he is a regular guy with whom readers should sympathize.

CHAPTER 4

WRITING TO MOVE OTHERS

The topics in this chapter revolve around issues of social injustice—prejudice, oppression, equality for women, and poverty. In many instances, the authors write about a situation they cannot control but one they feel strongly about. Today, it often appears as if students don't feel strongly about social issues; they are frequently charged with being apathetic. To test the truth of this, and simultaneously to generate topics, you can begin this chapter by accusing the students of apathy and asking them to defend themselves. Have them make a list of responses to questions like the following: What social issues do they feel strongly about? Which ones do they feel powerless to control? These questions may elicit some general responses, such as "acid rain" or "the depletion of the ozone layer." While these responses may be reassuring (yes, they *are* aware), they will be difficult to write about unless the students' feelings stem from personal involvement. So you need to take them to the next step.

Beside each item they have listed, have them jot down the gist of a personal experience that illustrates the problem or initiated their feelings. This exercise should yield more specific topics. But if it doesn't, you will need to take the students to yet another step. Ask them to list personal situations (but not too personal to share) over which they have no control; then list these items on the board. Now have them extrapolate—what social issues do these items illustrate?

This series of questions, answers, and discussion should prepare students for the readings in the chapter and generate topics to be explored in journal entries. When students are ready to begin selecting or developing a paper topic, ask them to read through their entries and classify them according to their purpose: Which ones could inspire a reader to persevere? Which ones illustrate a social injustice in such a way that the reader may be outraged? Which ones might inspire pity? Once this classification has been completed, students can decide which issues or experiences they feel most strongly about and then narrow the selection to the one with the most potential for development.

At this point, you can begin to have students experiment with language so that they can develop their style. As the authors of *Motives for Writing* point out, when one is writing to move a reader, style is extremely important. Have students bring in their first draft. In class, they can experiment with various introductions that will get the readers' attention and make them want to read on. In *From Sight to Insight*, Jeff Rackham and Olivia Bertagnolli suggest five different types of leads: the provocative lead, the contrast or conflict lead, the question lead, the cumulative interest lead, and the descriptive lead. Depending upon their focus and purpose, students can experiment with the lead most suited for their paper.

The provocative lead gets the reader's attention with an outrageous statement, such as "Boys are smarter than girls." The contrast or conflict lead establishes the focus of the paper by reversing the reader's expectations. It begins with a commonly accepted belief, then stands it on its head. The question lead is probably one of the most common but also one of the most abused. If students plan to use this strategy, they have to be sure that they don't raise rhetorical or unanswerable questions, such as "Is there life after death?" This type of question might best follow a descriptive lead, in which the author begins with an anecdote or describes a scene, then breaks to ask the reader, "Is this fair?" or "How many times has this happened to you?" Finally, the cumulative interest lead builds the reader's interest by piling up facts or details related to the upcoming story. A variation on Martin Luther King's speech, for instance, might open with a series of examples of prejudice. Taken alone, the examples would probably seem to be no more than inconveniences, but together, they show the reader how pervasive and destructive racism can be.

After introducing these leads to the students, you can have them experiment with the two or three that seem most appropriate for their paper. For more feedback, students can write different leads for their peers' papers after reading their drafts. All of this experimentation makes students aware of language and how it can affect their readers. With their consciousness raised, you can then have students work on style. Have either the authors or their peers select particularly effective passages from their drafts as models; then have them find weaker passages that can be revised or strengthened through the use of some of the rhetorical strategies used in this chapter—repetition, literary or biblical allusions, and parallel structure.

Further group work can deal with diction, focus, simplicity, or any other stylistic elements that make the students' writing more effective. For additional ideas and strategies, take a look at the Additional Writing Assignments at the end of the notes in this chapter.

Martin Luther King, Jr., "I Have a Dream"

Probably the best way to get students into this speech, to understand its power, is to play the recording of Dr. King reading it. After they listen to the record, have the students brainstorm comparisons of reading and hearing it. These two tasks should help demonstrate the power of persuasion to some degree, although they may not be sufficient to reach students who weren't born when he gave the speech. Another, more graphic approach is to use the tactic of dividing the students by eye or hair color when they enter the class and treating one group better than the other; for instance, make those with blue eyes sit in back, ignore everything they try to say, and outrageously reward anything the students in front have to say ("Oh, that deserves an A for today."). By the end of class, both groups will have caught on to what you're doing and why, but that will not lessen some feelings of resentment by those in the back. Capture those feelings and capitalize on them by having the students freewrite about their feelings; then in discussion, have them compare this brief experience to, say, two hundred years of discrimination.

George Orwell, "A Hanging"

Since both King and Orwell are writing about prejudice, tyranny, and oppression, you may want to assign these two essays together. Each is powerful and can be studied in its own right, but together, their differing forms transact to produce an even greater effect. At first, some students may not see the connection. Moreover, they will probably prefer Orwell because of the narrative format. A good place to start, then, is to assign a freewriting on which essay they preferred and why. Following a discussion of these freewritings and the essays' differences, ask students what the two have in common. This discussion is probably best done in groups of three or four so that students can share ideas and differing insights. Then you can point out the parallels between King and Ghandi, linking Ghandi to the British Empire and hence back to Orwell. One final strategy—which will make the oppression (and connections) most vivid—is to show films of southern lynchings, which can be found in civil rights documentaries.

Judy Syfers, "I Want a Wife"

This piece is usually fun to teach. The females understand and appreciate it; the males tend to squirm a little, and some will feel a bit maligned. A few students may not get the point. You can help them see its form and audience appeal by having groups work on putting it into a thesis/support format in a variation of the classic five-paragraph theme. This process should lead them to see the appeal of Syfers's ironic approach. You can then give equal time by having the males take the opposite stance: "I want a husband (or boyfriend.)" You may have to begin with the thesis/support format; otherwise, there will be some homophobics who will declare that *they* aren't "that kind of guy!" Once that threat, or misperception, is removed, students can write their own "I want a . . ." paper, either alone or in groups (groups provide the best results). When these pages are read aloud, the students may find that there are more damning details in Syfers's piece than in the essays considering the other side, which will bring to light the validity of her argument.

Alice Walker, "Am I Blue?"

This essay raises a number of issues. To reveal them, it may be helpful to begin class with a freewriting asking students what Walker's point is. What is she arguing about—and how do they know? The responses should lead into a discussion not only of issues but also of rhetorical strategies and matters of style. A second line of inquiry is to ask, Were you moved? How did you feel after reading this piece? What part(s) affected you most? What did that part remind you of or make you want to change? This move into reader response personalizes the essay (and provides ideas for their own paper), while making students further aware of how effective Walker is. If these strategies aren't enough to make the students aware of this form of persuasion, you can revert to the five-paragraph theme strategy referred to earlier; take this beautiful essay apart and put it into that format. How does this form affect its appeal?

Randall Williams, "Daddy Tucked the Blanket"

While this piece may elicit pity, it probably won't gain the students' empathy or understanding. As Williams says, "You have to live it to understand it." Moreover, although he points out that his parents worked hard and that they weren't shiftless, most students unconsciously believe in social Darwinism—that you can move up in the world if you want to. This belief is confirmed by the fact that Williams *did* move up and out. So how do you overcome these prejudices? You can start with his statement that "other children can be incredibly cruel." The students can freewrite about a time when they were the object of such cruelty. After students share their sketches, you can discuss why the children in the freewriting were cruel and how the situations were resolved. Then compare their situations with Williams's to show how he was caught in his environment. Once this understanding is established and the situation is humanized, you can move back to the essay to discuss what parts or details (beyond the obvious— the title) show the humanity and futility of the situation and the people involved.

Jonathan Swift, "A Modest Proposal"

Whenever I teach this essay, I find there are usually at least two or three students who have taken it literally and are sickened or outraged. Since the emphasis in this section is on moving others, you may want to begin the class by asking students to freewrite their response to this reading—what did they like or dislike and why? This response will show you their reading ability and engage them with both content and style. Once the secret is out, you can ask at what point they realized the essay was satirical. This discussion will move the focus onto Swift's organization and development. A logical follow-up is to ask students to brainstorm current social issues worthy of such treatment and then have them choose one and develop their own "modest proposal." Reading these essays aloud will demonstrate how satire and humor can move audiences more easily than fire and brimstone.

ADDITIONAL WRITING ASSIGNMENTS

1. *A situation beyond my control.* Orwell and Walker move their audience by telling a story about a situation over which they had no control. Both use seemingly personal narratives to make a point about a larger social issue. The readings in this chapter may have elicited memories of a number of similar situations from your life. Make a list of possibilities and choose the one you can remember the most about and/or feel strongest about. Using the narrative format, tell about this experience, employing details and descriptions that will move the reader to understand the larger point you are making.

2. *Social issues.* Syfers and Swift use irony and satire to make a point about social issues in need of change—the inequality of marriage and the insensitivity of government, respectively. These approaches, through their use of humor, can often move audiences more effectively than direct appeals. What social issues do you feel strongly about? What would you like to see changed? To organize and develop your ideas, divide a sheet of paper in half. List the issues you'd like changed on one side and some outrageous solutions opposite them on the other side. Once you have decided on a topic, try clustering ideas to come up with ways to develop your solution. You may want to directly emulate Swift's or Syfers's approach. If so, an outline of the essay's organization will help you arrange your points in an equally effective manner.

3. *Oppression.* King, Orwell, Syfers, and Walker all talk about oppression, yet each develops his or her discussion differently. If you have not already dealt with this topic in a previous writing exercise, you may want to take a different approach. Dr. King differs from the others in his use of biblical passages and emulation of famous orations and oratorical styles to move his audience to action. This style appealed to the members of his primarily black audience, who were raised in southern Baptist churches. If this approach appeals to you, decide on what element of oppression you'd like to discuss, who your audience would be, and what historical or rhetorical documents you want to model your argument on. This technique will probably entail a trip to the library

ANSWERS TO QUESTIONS

King, "I Have a Dream"

1. Since Lincoln wrote the Emancipation Proclamation that freed the slaves, the setting is particularly appropriate. King alludes to Lincoln when he begins his second paragraph with "Five score years ago," similar to the beginning of the Gettysburg Address.

2. See the answer to Question 1.

3. In paragraph 5, "Now is the time"; in paragraph 8, "We cannot"; in paragraph 10, "Go back to"; in paragraphs 11–13, "I have a dream"; in paragraphs 16–17, "Let freedom ring."

4. If people see that change is occurring, even gradually, they may become content to let things move slowly.

5. Dr. King was a minister, so he was very familiar with the Bible.

6. His admonition against violence suggests his awareness of the feeling of urgency for change. He also uses "we" to show that they are all on the same

side. To lift up the hearts of his listeners, he uses the techniques of the southern Baptist minister—exhortations, repetition through anaphora, quotations from the Bible.

Orwell, "A Hanging"

1. Sodden rains and "a sickly light" paint a depressing scene. The description of the cells as "small animal cages" elicits sympathy for the men who are held in them.

2. Orwell contrasts the relative helplessness of the condemned man to his huge captors by likening the scene to "men handling a fish which is still alive and may jump back into the water."

3. The appearance and behavior of the dog brings a note of reality into the hanging. The dog's antics show how truly alive it is; his licking of the prisoner's face reminds the soldiers that the condemned is also a human being.

4. The condemned man's avoidance of the puddle shows that he still has feelings and life: "he was alive just as we are alive."

5. The prayer reminds the listeners that what they are doing is breaking the Commandments. The bell-like consistency of the man's calls could be an allusion to a bell's death knells, as in Donne's line, "Never send to know for whom the bell tolls; it tolls for thee."

6. Orwell observes that the men watching "had changed color"; the act made them sick.

7. Many readers do not realize that this is more than a "story," yet they are moved by the action and description. Even if readers have a limited knowledge of England's rule in Burma, they are still moved by these events.

Syfers, "I Want a Wife"

1. The title is effective because the author's name is immediately below it.

2. The refrain "I want, I want," is often associated with the whining of a selfish child. But in this case, it emphasizes a woman's rebellion into self-assertions after self-denial.

3. Syfers probably would not want to perpetuate this master-slave life-style; she writes about it to point out its injustice and society's acceptance of it.

4. Syfers is feeling more anger at the injustice than self-pity. She knows she can do all these things herself.

5. My students' first reaction is that this piece is indeed dated; the boys particularly believe this. They always state that relationships are no longer

like this—even though their parents fulfill many of the same roles. As discussion continues, it becomes clear that expectations have not changed that much. The boys acknowledge that since most wives work now, the work load is divided somewhat, but there is still not an equal division of duties.

Walker, "Am I Blue?"

1. Walker's description may be establishing a theme of appearance versus reality or a theme of one not needing to worry about something if one is unaware of it.

2. The horse's name symbolizes its feelings, but by identifying the horse by a color, she also introduces the element of prejudice and identification with its feelings, as suggested in one reading of the title. Her descriptions of the horse's eyes elicit the most sympathy.

3. See the answer to Question 2.

4. There can be different connotations attached to these words. "Companion" and "partner" are used by some people to identify a person of the same sex whom they live with. They can also suggest that two people of the opposite sex are living together without being married. Using "friend" to describe the other horse seems to go beyond either of these connotations; it suggests that the two horses are more than sex partners. Walker is personalizing the horse.

5. I have seen, in the eyes of my animals, different emotions that reflect their moods, so I believe that Blue would and could show emotions. Walker then uses these specific emotions as a metaphor for larger feelings.

6. Walker integrates the larger issues fairly smoothly. If they were stuck on at the end, they would not be nearly as effective. They would seem like an afterthought rather than an integral part of the whole story.

7. I don't think Walker has turned into a vegetarian. She has lost her appetite after thinking about blindness and injustice. Spitting symbolizes the extent of her feelings.

Williams, "Daddy Tucked the Blanket"

1. Adult readers may understand what Williams is trying to convey, but students may have a more difficult time. They grew up in an era of social Darwinism. As a result, they have difficulty believing that the poor should be pitied and that their situation is not their fault.

2. The short paragraphs serve as exclamation points; they get the reader's attention.

3. Williams clarifies the purpose of these paragraphs when he writes, "I tell you this to show that we weren't shiftless." He gives background to aid understanding.

4. The girls had to help with the housework, which was a more difficult task. They also had to meet their dates at home, which was embarrassing. Although he doesn't mention it, clothing would probably be more difficult for girls, too—keeping it clean and pressed and fashionable.

5. Williams attributes his parents' divorce to the anger they expressed to each other about their living conditions. He doesn't seem to blame either one for the poverty or the divorce.

6. Williams may have been grateful for that moment because it made him aware of the need for forgiveness, tolerance, and understanding; or it may have hardened his resolve to break out of this world of poverty.

Swift, "A Modest Proposal"

1. This answer will probably vary according to one's reading strengths, but for me it occurred at the end of paragraph 4 when Swift states that instead of being a burden, "they shall on the contrary contribute to the feeding, and partly to the clothing, of many thousands."

2. Swift builds his argument slowly, he points out its advantages, and he supports his arguments with statistics and with attacks on straw men, such as papists, the government, and barbaric Americans.

3. Adolescent boys' flesh is too tough and lean; the females would soon be breeders themselves. Swift isn't concerned about the elderly poor because they die off on their own.

4. Because of British domination, the Irish were starving. The economic situation caused many Protestants to emigrate. The country was dependent upon England for imports and income, and consequently, it had no self-pride or patriotism.

5. Swift wants the government to come up with a better plan to feed and clothe the poor; he makes his argument to bring their plight to the government's attention. Note that he mentions a number of alternatives in paragraph 29.

6. The last paragraph reiterates the dire state of the nation, while ending on a humorous note to appeal to the reader.

7. Swift is writing to shock. By taking an extreme stance, he can hope to point out how serious the problem is and, at the very least, move his readers and the government toward a more humane solution.

CHAPTER 5

WRITING TO PERSUADE OTHERS

With this motive, persuasion, the writing assignments become more structured. That doesn't mean, however, that they should suddenly be divorced from the students' interest or experience. To determine where their interests lie, have students write about one of the social issues discussed in this chapter—sports, drugs, English only, death penalty, homosexuality, an individual's constitutional rights—they feel most strongly about and tell why. Those students who are uninterested in these issues can write instead about something they'd like to change within their social milieu.

Once students have selected a topic, have them freewrite everything they know and feel about it. Then to generate additional material and to teach them to recognize the need to address counterarguments, have them write an argumentative dialogue between themselves and an informed opponent. The first step in this assignment is to label every assertion made in the initial freewriting. This is side A. On a separate sheet of paper, have students write down each assertion and then refute it in the persona of side B—an anonymous adversary or a known one (such as father, teacher, priest—whoever disagrees). This method of point-counterpoint should help them see any fallacies in their own arguments and further strengthen their position to overcome them. It also provides a clear argumentative purpose and approach—to change their reader's mind. For further input, you could have students find an article that argues the opposite point of view and have them continue the dialogue with its author.

When students have clarified their stance, they can decide how to persuade their reader: through appeal to emotion, to character, or to logic, or through a combination of appeals. That decided, they will need to organize their argument. Whatever approach they choose, they will then need to develop backing, either through illustrations and examples or through references to authorities on the subject. At this point, you can refer them to their original assertions and use them as a source for daily journal entries. For each assertion, have students write an extended illustration or example, or find and summarize an authoritative source. This exercise should provide students with sufficient backing to effectively persuade their readers.

All of this material will eventually need to be organized into a cohesive, coherent, and persuasive essay. To help students determine the organizational structure that is most effective, have them analyze the organization of the essays in this chapter. Designate seven groups, one for each essay, and have each group map its essay's organization. These maps can then be written on the board and used as models. If you have enough time, you can have students experiment with more than one organizational model to determine which would be most effective for their argument. This combination of written models and organizational maps should help students produce well-organized arguments.

Estelle Gilson, "Down with Mother's Day"

It's hard to gauge possible reactions to this reading. While most students would probably agree that women's roles have changed, they would also see this proposal as a sacrilege—Mother's Day has always been observed, so it should continue to be. A good way to determine reactions (and give students practice in persuasion) is to have them freewrite a response from the ready-made thesis: "I agree/disagree that Mother's Day should go because. . . ." To illustrate how to develop an argument, divide the "agrees" and "disagrees" into groups of three or four and have them synthesize their reasons into a larger argument. To illustrate organization, have one side put its reasons on the board, and then have the other side refute with its counterarguments. Rhetorical strategies can then be taught by having them rearrange the arguments, building from weakest to strongest. The obvious follow-up is to have them argue "Down with Father's Day."

Louis Barbash, "Clean Up or Pay Up"

Few students will disagree with this argument; however, not everyone will be able to follow its organization. To help them see the author's reasoning, divide the students into groups and have them map the progression of arguments. A visual map often makes these patterns easier to understand and model. Once the organization is clear, you can take one of two directions. Discuss what makes Barbash's argument persuasive; most would agree that the introduction, plus similar examples throughout, is very powerful. With the argument's organization and persuasive strategies clear, you can have students apply what they've learned—have them refute it. A second approach is to have students brainstorm a list of readers who would fight these changes, select one, and freewrite an opposing argument from that person's point of view, following the pattern already modeled. Analyzing techniques and then applying them should make writing their own arguments a little easier.

Mark A. R. Kleiman, "Snowed In"

This essay may be a little more difficult for students to relate to. Although they may agree that drugs, especially cocaine, are a problem, they may not be very interested in the big picture. To bring this problem closer to home, have them freewrite about someone they know who has a problem with drugs (including alcohol, nicotine, and steroids), describing that person's problem and then suggesting possible solutions. Since Kleiman's argument is developed by offering various solutions and showing why they don't work, you can teach this strategy inductively by doing the same thing with the students' freewritings. Survey the entire class, having each student give one solution offered in his or her freewriting. Write the solution on the board; then ask why it wouldn't work. As the possible solutions pile up and are discarded, students should begin to see the magnitude of the drug problem and the difficulty of solving it. At the same time, Kleiman's persuasive strategies should become clearer.

Yolanda T. De Mola, "The Language of Power"

You may want to assign this essay in conjunction with Richard Rodriguez's and Barbara Mellix's, since they support and illustrate De Mola's point. But that probably isn't enough to make students care about it. Compared with drugs, sports, and Mother's Day, this topic lacks pizazz—who would disagree? Who, in fact, is really interested in English, as a language or a class? This may be a good place to start. A quick poll of the class will probably reveal a general boredom with the subject. At most, they will agree with De Mola that "far greater benefits might be reaped by the 1.5 million children with a limited knowledge of English if creative and intensive English programs were to be offered to them." Ask students to do a freewriting on the reasons why English is boring—why, despite the fact that it is the "language of power," few people want to take English courses and few, including native speakers, do well. Follow up by asking how English as a subject could be made creative and interesting, or how some people come to excel so that for them it does become a source of power. These freewritings can make the topic personally relevant; at the same time, they will give students more practice in argumentative and persuasive writing.

Edward I. Koch, "Death and Justice"

Most students today will agree with this argument. Possibly the easiest way to approach this reading is to ask them to write about why they agree with Koch. If there is anyone who disagrees, you can use these two opposing viewpoints to model yet another argument paper, following Koch's paradigm of argument-counterargument. Because so many students agree with capital punishment, you may want to take this argument a step farther, into analysis. This can be done by linking Koch's essay with Kleiman's article on drugs. Koch points out that "in America the murder rate climbed 122 percent between 1963 and 1980. During that same period, the murder rate in New York City increased by almost 400 percent. . . ." This period marks the beginning and growing popularity of drug use. Is there cause and effect? Recent studies have shown that the majority of prison inmates are substance abusers, although most often the substance abused is alcohol. What arguments can the students make by drawing on these statistics?

Jacob Weisberg, "Gays in Arms"

If students have already dealt with Groff's "Taking the Test" (Chapter 1), they may be slightly less homophobic—perhaps. No matter what level of paranoia they exhibit, they should find the military's arguments specious. One way to find out is to ask for a written response to the statement that "homosexuality is incompatible with military service." Ask students to begin by defining what "military service" means to them and to move from there into its relation to, or incompatability with, homosexuality. To illustrate possible weaknesses in the students' definitions, you can then ask them to respond to the policy that women should not serve in combat. If they correlate homosexuality with feminine traits, you can counter that opinion with the judgment that women make excellent soldiers. Nevertheless, "women are dismissed for homosexuality three times as often as men are, eight times as often in the Marine Corps." Have them explain those statistics. This series of arguments should lead the more mature students to see the illogic of the military's stance. At that point, you might ask why military men are so extremely homophobic. Responses to this question can be put in the form of yet another argument, to give students further practice in persuasion.

Thomas Jefferson, "The Declaration of Independence"

This piece falls at an excellent spot. It can be used to evaluate and analyze the essays in this chapter. Does paragraph 2 apply to the issues of women's and athletes' rights, drug laws, bilingual education, capital punishment, or gay rights? Ask students to pick one of these issues (or another of their choice from current events) and show how it does or does not conform to those self-evident truths. A second application of the Declaration is to have students compare the charges against the king with recent actions of the president or Supreme Court. Does the United States still follow the precepts on which the Declaration was based? To manage this, you will probably have to divide the twenty-nine paragraphs dealing with the king between groups of four or five students each. When all the groups have finished and presented their findings, the ensuing discussion can lead to a persuasive argument in answer to the above question, organized along the lines of Jefferson's.

ADDITIONAL WRITING ASSIGNMENTS

1. *Change.* All of the authors in this chapter argue for some type of change. Some arguments are more persuasive than others, partly because of how they are written, but also because of how pertinent their topic is to the reader. Both points need to be taken into account when you are writing a persuasive paper. Choose an interesting topic and make it persuasive by incorporating equally interesting illustrations and examples. Given these criteria, consider what things you'd like to change. Of these, what would be interesting to an audience of your peers? How would you get their interest and hold it? Write a persuasive paper that advocates a particular change. Model your organization on the essay in this chapter you find most persuasive.

2. *Individual rights.* Weisberg, Jefferson, and, to some extent, Gilson all write about an individual's rights—Weisberg about gays, Jefferson about Americans, and Gilson about women. What rights do you feel strongly about? On what issues would you argue if your personal rights were denied? Make a list of rights you cherish, and then decide what people might infringe upon them and how you would persuade them to leave you alone, or to drop the issue if they are making it public policy. Each of the authors mentioned above uses a persuasive strategy appropriate to his or her purpose and audience. Decide which strategies would be most persuasive for

your argument; feel free to draw upon those used by the other authors in
this section as well.

3. *A personal issue.* Even if you are a concerned citizen, the topics discussed
    in this chapter may not be ones you feel a need to write about. Instead, you
    may want to apply the persuasive strategies to a more personally relevant
    writing assignment. Who do you need to persuade right now: Your parents?
    A teacher? A company? A pro-lifer? An angry friend? Make a list of people
    who might be persuaded to change their mind if you wrote to them. Then
    choose one person and decide what strategy would best be suited for this
    writing situation. Once you have written a draft, you may find that you can
    apply additional strategies to make your argument more powerful. Feel free
    to rewrite your argument. The more you revise, the better your paper will be.

ANSWERS TO QUESTIONS

Gilson, "Down with Mother's Day"

1. By stating her claim in the first sentence, Gilson immediately gets the
    readers' attention. Whether they agree or disagree, they will probably want
    to read on to discover why she would say such an outrageous thing. The
    only disadvantage might be that some readers would find her statement so
    ridiculous that they would refuse to read on.

2. Gilson thinks there is no need for Mother's Day because mothers
    supposedly no longer have to work as hard as when the holiday was
    established, thanks to the development of modern science and technology.

3. By cramming a series of details into these sentences, Gilson shows the
    extent of a mother's work. If she broke up these sentences, the effect might
    be lost because the reading would be choppy and more tedious. You can
    only effectively use long lists once or twice.

4. Readers' reactions to this statement will probably depend on their gender
    and their mothers. If they had controlling mothers, or even perceived them
    as such, they will agree. If they didn't, then they should see that this is a
    fairly broad generalization.

5. Gilson recognizes two extremes—the very rich and the very poor working
    mother. There are many other types in between that just don't fit these
    stereotypes. Moreover, she ignores the fact that the majority of women work
    because they have to; there is no extra money for frills.

6. This essay would not have been accepted if it had been written by a man;
    even written by a woman, it is extremely sexist. That Gilson is a
    grandmother may explain her stance. Motherhood may have been much
    more difficult for her in the years when she was starting a family than it is

for similar mothers today. Because she is now a grandmother, she may not be aware of the different types of difficulties women have to contend with.

Barbash, "Clean Up or Pay Up"

1. Barbash's introduction illustrates the lure and the reality of college athletics. Too many athletes believe that sports is a ticket to the good life, failing to realize that only a few make it professionally.

2. Colleges recruit and admit unqualified students and use their athletic ability for four years to sell tickets and television time; few worry about the students' education. Schools offer scholarships with the implicit promise that a college education will enable students to become professional athletes. To ensure eligibility, schools concoct easy or nonexistent courses that the students can pass but that do not educate them.

3. Students can't be drafted until they are in college. Only one in 400 is drafted because there are only so many slots per year open on the pro teams.

4. Anyone who is familiar with professional athletics and the college programs that produce the players will believe this argument. There just aren't that many teams. The problem is that too many of the nondrafted and nongraduating players are invisible; we see only the few who succeed.

5. Barbash outlines the advantages of paying athletes: It would create thousands of new jobs; students would get paid during their years of apprenticeship; they could wait until they were mature enough to attend college; they would have more time to study and practice; and they could take courses they were genuinely interested in. The disadvantage seems to be that this program might lead to even fewer students getting educated than at present, for it's doubtful that the majority of the students who never graduate have any real interest in college. Not forced to go, they won't.

6. The pun refers to "poetry or prose." This sentence sets up the two options that would be made available: Either study or go professional—not both at once.

Kleiman, "Snowed In"

1. "Cocaine isn't scarce and can't be made scarce."

2. The government has tried interdiction, seizing shipments, burning fields, arresting dealers, arresting users, and passing laws. None of their methods have worked because supply and demand remain.

3. Seizing drug shipments only enables suppliers to raise the price, claiming scarcity.

4. Kleiman maintains that punishing drug dealers—his solution—offers "some hope of actually reducing the impact of drug dealing on our lives." He

builds to his solution, debunking alternatives so that his is the only one left. He precedes his solution by pointing out why politicians won't like it, but he clings to it as the only hope.

5. Kleiman's solution reveals him to be fairly conservative—he believes in punishment, not education. He seems concerned about the amount of money the government is wasting on interdiction, but he apparently sees no problems in putting the money into more prisons.

De Mola, "The Language of Power"

1. Neither of these arguments is particularly persuasive. The first one is not really debatable, and her closing example leaves her open to counterarguments.

2. De Mola argues implicitly that bilingual classes take away money that would be better spent on developing better English teachers and courses. She states directly that, at least in the Bronx, the bilingual program is a "'dumping ground' for kids with limited English proficiency," which suggests that they become labeled and stuck in their own language.

3. By *integration*, De Mola implies that Hispanics have become a part of American society, but they have not been assimilated—they still are seen as different and are victims of prejudice. If schools become integrated, all races will attend. That does not mean, however, that the minorities will have been accepted—that is, *assimilated.*

4. De Mola uses a mixed analogy here. She has been arguing for the assimilation of Hispanics into American culture, yet her example cites American tourists. Moreover, an advocate for bilingualism could point out that most non-Americans are bilingual because English is taught in their country.

Koch, "Death and Justice"

1. I think Koch's strategy is to show readers that these killers came to this belief only because they were faced with their own deaths. He does not quote them to elicit sympathy; he believes readers will see how these men have learned their lesson.

2. Koch cites his experience to suggest that he has carefully weighed all the evidence before coming to his conclusions.

3. His statement that capital punishment is analogous with chemotherapy is specious, as is his claim that we need the death penalty because we have more murders; his claim that it is not discriminatory simply ignores the facts. Possibly his most persuasive argument is that the death penalty eliminates the chance of multiple murders.

4. On moral issues, it is very difficult to use refutation to prove one's case. However, refutation is a strong rhetorical strategy in writing. Usually, however, it should be combined with other strategies rather than relied upon to the extent that Koch has used it here.

5. There are repeat offenders in New York for the same reason that they exist all over the country—the prisons are overcrowded and do little or nothing to educate or rehabilitate the inmates.

6. When murderers are not punished, victims can be said to die twice because their rights have been denied during the crime and again when there is no retribution.

Weisberg, "Gays in Arms"

1. In 1982, the military elaborated its rules to cover all the bases. Because the rules are so general, military personnel can use them to justify getting rid of any gay person, whether or not that person has actually done anything suspect.

2. The 1982 rules spell out the arguments: The presence of gays affects morale, disrupts discipline and order; lessens the dignity, trust, and confidence among members and the integrity of rank; affects public perception and the ability to recruit new members; and heightens the threat of security breaches.

3. The Crittenden report "recommended that the military continue to exclude homosexuals," even though it showed that they were not security risks and performed their duties as well as heterosexuals. The military suppresses such reports because it doesn't want to change its policies or leave the armed forces open to lawsuits.

4. Since women are in the minority in the armed services, their behavior can be more easily noticed and scrutinized. Since the military does not want women to serve, they will use any excuse to get rid of them. Also, because of stereotypical gender roles, there may be a presumption (Would a "real" woman want to be a soldier?) that leads to prejudicial judgments.

5. In his conclusion, Weisberg notes that "support for the policy appears to be weakening," since a recent study found that 92 percent of the American public did not believe homosexuality should be grounds for discharge.

6. This analogy is useful because both groups are discriminated against solely through ignorance; moreover, experience has shown that prejudice against black soldiers was groundless and successfully overcome in time.

Jefferson, "The Declaration of Independence"

1. Jefferson uses "men" generically to mean all human beings. "Unalienable rights" cannot be transferred or taken away. "The pursuit of happiness" does not mean fun and games; it means a general freedom to be treated decently.

2. When Jefferson says governments derive their powers "from the consent of the governed," he overlooks the influence of the electoral college, which makes the general voter's views invalid. While he notes that it is the right of the people "to alter or to abolish" a government that "becomes destructive of these ends," the Supreme Court's influence is not taken into account.

3. Probably the most serious is the billeting of armies among the citizens. That is the most threatening and intrusive.

4. The American Indians' needs or rights to their lands were ignored; they weren't considered as people, so they were not seen as "men created equal," and therefore had no unalienable rights. Note the racist reference to "merciless Indian savages" in paragraph 29.

5. Jefferson constructs his arguments slowly and rationally so that they will not appear to be rash. Note his reference to earlier petitions in paragraph 30.

6. By leaving "united" uncapitalized, the states seem to be a number of separate bodies in agreement; capitalizing "United" presents them as one body, one country.

CHAPTER 6

WRITING TO CONVEY INFORMATION

Like the first five motives for writing, writing to convey information demands the writer's interest and knowledge. But writing to inform is especially pertinent to the students' work in other classes. So you may want to use the strategies and rhetorical approaches in these essays as models for students to develop their papers in other classes. At the very least, you can offer this as an option.

Despite your largesse, some students will prefer to write on something that really interests them—something they know a lot about or wish to explore. To develop potential journal and paper topics, ask them to make three lists: things they're good at; people, things, or issues they're curious about; and things they have to write about. The lucky student will have items that overlap on each list. Most others, however, will have to make a choice. This choice should be based upon interest. Have them rank all the items from the three lists and then zero in on the top three or four.

Using these items as topics, have students conduct an "I-Search" on each. Developed by Ken Macrorie (and explained in more detail in his *Telling Writing*), the I-Search has students write everything they know and want to know about a subject. This task helps them generate personal knowledge, while it simultaneously provides a focus for research—their research will furnish answers to their questions. After completing an I-Search for each of their top-ranked topics, students should know which one they wish to pursue with research. Help students organize their research by having them brainstorm a list of potential sources of information. What will they read? Who can they interview?

Once their research tasks have been determined, you can help students develop the necessary writing skills by having them create summaries and generate interview questions. Summary skills can best be taught by having the students summarize the essays in this chapter. Brenda Spatt's *Writing from Sources* provides clear steps for teaching the summary. You can help students sharpen their skills by having them begin with a one-page summary; then have them narrow it to a paragraph and, finally, to a single statement. When you feel students have learned to summarize, they can apply these skills to the articles they find in the library that pertain to their topics, summarizing them in their journals or turning in daily summaries of their findings.

The notes in this manual offer various suggestions for helping students develop their interview skills. You may want to prepare them initially by having them analyze the essays that are built on interview information. In groups, have the students infer (and write down) the questions that must have been asked to develop these essays. This exercise helps them model the interview process and the types of questions necessary to elicit useful information. It also provides a focus for the students' own interviews. They can decide what types of questions will be most pertinent and in what order they should occur.

Needless to say, all of these tasks will generate a large body of data that students will need to organize. To do so, they will also need to analyze and classify it. What types of information have they found? What would work well in an introduction? Can the information be organized into a narrative, or would it work better as comparison-contrast or cause-effect? The answers to these questions will depend upon the focus and purpose of the paper. Yet the students may not be entirely sure of the focus until they have analyzed all the material.

To help them gain some perspective, have them reread their original I-Search. What did they already know? What have they learned? One way to help them organize the information they find in the library is to provide periodic (daily or weekly) synthesis sessions. In these sessions, have them divide a paper into two columns. On the left side, they should list their original ideas or the points they plan to make. Opposite each point, have them list the library source that supports or refutes that idea. By doing this on a regular basis, they will know where to integrate or introduce their secondary sources before they begin writing. This step should make drafting much easier.

Once students have completed their synthesis, they should write a rough draft. This draft can be an expansion of their original I-Search freewriting. The students' original knowledge will serve as the introduction, and their questions can be organized into a logical order to provide an outline for inserting the new information. For student writers at this level, just organizing and inserting the information may be a good deal of work. In fact, it may be so overwhelming that it cancels out any objectivity. To help them regain perspective, have students exchange drafts and answer some basic questions about their peers' papers: What is the author's thesis? What is the scope of the paper? What is the background or purpose of this research? Then have the peer editors list the topics covered to see whether they follow a pattern of increasing importance or whether they fall into one of the other organizational patterns. Final work can focus on the conclusion. From reading it, the editor should be able to tell what the author has learned.

This collaborative work should help students revise their first draft; subsequent sessions can focus on logic, style, mechanics, and documentation.

Sam Bingham, "A Share of the River"

You will need to relate the essays in this chapter directly to the students' experience, both personal and academic, in order to engage them in the reading and to make them appreciate its relevance. As a type of exposition, writing to convey information is the type they do most often for other classes. As Bingham's essay shows, this type of writing entails some degree of research, either primary or secondary. You might begin the discussion by asking students what type of class this writing would be appropriate for. That puts it into a relevant context. Then you can introduce students to this essay by having them do a freewriting comparing their hometown (or neighborhood where they grew up) as it was when they were children with how it is now. They can use Bingham's piece as a model. In groups, have the students map or outline the essay's parts to see what types of details are covered in each "half" of the comparison-contrast. Put the maps on the board for reference during the freewriting. A discussion of the finished freewritings should lead the students to see the necessity for different types of research to develop this piece.

Raymond Sokolov, "The Dark Side of Tomatoes"

This essay can be linked with Bingham's, since both present information in a comparison-contrast format. You can begin by telling students that and then asking them (again) to map or outline the organization of the piece. Whereas Bingham uses before-after, Sokolov uses perception-reality. Awareness of these similar structures should show students that both essays also have similar and relevant purposes—both could be used in academic settings. Of course, although this information is useful, it isn't fascinating; it most likely will not be sufficient to get them involved. To help students assimilate this organizational format, ask them to generate a list of topics that fall into the category of perception-reality, where knowledge has replaced earlier misperceptions, either personal or scientific. These lists, plus the freewritings that would naturally follow, should be interesting and possibly entertaining. In both cases, the freewritings should again lead to the realization that additional research is necessary to present a convincing and fully developed case.

Elizabeth Kaye, "Peter Jennings Gets No Self-Respect"

Although this piece is longer than others in the chapter, students will probably like it best—it's fast, interesting, and current, like an article in *People* magazine. They may want to emulate its style, even though it seems particularly irrelevant to academic writing. Nevertheless, since the implicit emphasis in this chapter has been on the necessity of research, you can teach interview skills by having them determine the kinds and sources of information used in this article. Then they can make a list of people they'd like to interview. Since this essay is about a man and his job, you can have them interview someone with a job they'd like to have or plan to have upon graduation. The students can work in groups developing interview questions or even sharing sources; they can also practice interviews on each other and freewrite the results to see whether their questions were adequate. In other words, the work done for this essay, like the other papers for this chapter, can be solid preparation for a larger paper.

John Sedgwick, "The Doberman Case"

This reading could be linked with Walker's "Am I Blue?" from Chapter 4, since both evoke great feeling for animals through description and demonstrate how similar animals and humans are—something we don't always recognize or respect. But obviously, "The Doberman Case" goes into much more detail, it has a different purpose, and it follows a more complex organizational pattern than "Am I Blue?" does. Rather than telling the students all of this, have them tell you. If the two essays are assigned together (or on consecutive days), open the class by having small groups determine why you assigned them, what the purpose of each is, and how their organization and use of details accomplish that purpose. This type of inductive reasoning is often more effective than a straight lecture. Once the context has been established, you can become more specific, asking the rhetorical purpose of the "case of Blue" and the "Doberman case" in each article. (Blue has layers of meaning, while the Doberman provides a neat frame and engaging introduction.) If you see an investigative report as one option for this chapter, you can end this class by asking the students what topics they would like to investigate and how the organization of this piece would apply to their own paper.

Dennis Farney, "Inside Hallmark's Love Machine"

This essay works well with Sedgwick's, since both look at the functioning of a company and both use topic-related anecdotes to frame the research. To prepare students for this reading, have them do a freewriting that tells what kind of cards they buy, for whom, how often, and for how much (on average). Then correlate the responses to what Farney found in his research. This discussion may then lead into an analysis of the type of research done for this piece— where you go, who and what you ask—which can be done within small groups. Once that information is established, you may want to return to the list of topics for research and ask students what companies they would like to research and why.

Nicholas Lemann, "Stressed Out in Suburbia"

You may wish to assign this piece along with "A Share of the River," since both focus on a place and related social issues and both organize the discussion by using comparison-contrast (although that organization isn't quite as obvious in this essay, since it's point by point). If you want to broaden the discussion and provide an additional model, you might also assign "Growing Up Stoned" by Elizabeth Kaye, which looks at a California suburb to discuss the effects of the drug culture. To prepare students for the discussion, have them freewrite a description of their hometown or suburb, comparing it with Naperville. This writing can be done at the beginning of class, prior to any discussion, or after the organizational pattern is discerned. At that point, they can use this piece as a model and organize their freewriting point by point. As a follow-up, have them ask their parents to read their freewritings and compare that same place with what it was when they grew up. As they write, you need to make students aware that their comparison should have a purpose. Why was "Stressed Out" or "A Share" written? What point will they make by comparing their suburb or hometown now with the way it used to be? Once they realize the necessity of a purpose, they can narrow the focus to details that illustrate and support it.

Stephen Jay Gould, "Women's Brains"

Prior to assigning this piece, you might give students a quotation from Broca's "chief misogynist," Le Bon, and have them freewrite a response to it. Then assign the essay and ask them to compare their initial response with what they found in the essay. This type of assignment will engage their interest, focus their reading, and improve comprehension. This piece parallels Sokolov's;

Gould takes a misperception and debunks it through research. Rather than point this out, ask students to tell you how they are similar. Building on these similarities, you can refer them to their initial lists (of misperceptions-realities) and ask them to add to the lists. Or they can proceed with the male-female misperceptions and develop a list that can be used as a focus for research.

ADDITIONAL WRITING ASSIGNMENTS

1. *Write about a place.* Bingham and Lemann write comparison-contrast pieces about towns. Bingham's purpose is to discuss environmental issues; Lemann focuses on the cultural issues (or lack thereof). If this approach interests you, decide what place you'd like to write about, what you want your audience to learn about it, what point you plan to make, and how you will gain any additional information you may need. As these authors' work demonstrates, you should choose a place you are familiar with so that you can draw on firsthand knowledge; or you should choose a place nearby if you want to get firsthand observations and interview inhabitants. By going to the site of your research, you may also be able to get access to the town's archives; these documents can lend additional depth to your report.

2. *Write about a person.* The preliminary work done in conjunction with reading about Peter Jennings may have convinced you that this type of informative writing is the most interesting or is pertinent to your future career. Depending on your purpose in writing, decide on who you plan to write about and whether you will need to gain additional information by interviewing that person. If you plan to include information from an interview, contact your subject to set up one or a series of interview dates. Remember that the person is doing you a favor, so make the appointment at his or her convenience (although you may have some possible dates already selected to make the decision easier and mutually convenient). When the groundwork has been laid, develop your interview questions and organize them into a logical sequence. Try to arrive at the site early so that you can take notes on your subject's surroundings, which may help to define the person. Following the interview, write up your impressions or flesh out any notes while the information is still fresh. When you begin to write, you may use Elizabeth Kaye's "Peter Jennings" essay as a model.

3. *Write about a controversial issue.* Sokolov and Gould headed for the library and conducted their own research to resolve misperceptions. Although tomatoes and women's brains have nothing in common (despite Broca's opinions), the forms of the two articles do. Both are comparison-contrast based on myth or misperception and reality. From the class discussions, you may want to continue or expand upon research about male-female differences, or you may branch off into an area that interests you, either conducting your own research (via interviews or surveys) or drawing upon published research in the library. As you select a topic, keep in mind that this research strategy is a useful one to use for papers in other classes as

well. If your teachers agree, you may want to use this assignment and organizational strategy to develop a research paper for another course.

ANSWERS TO QUESTIONS

Bingham, "A Share of the River"

1. Because it sold most of its water rights, Rocky Ford has "sunk so low in the food chain of the state economy" that it lost the rest of them, too. As a result, the community has become "half dead."

2. Ron Aschermann's son represents the demise of the American farming family; because of big business, farming is impossible, so the son is learning another trade. Meanwhile, the Bowlen family has made so much money from the farmers' water that it can afford to buy a sports team. These facts show how unjust the sale was.

3. Tom Griswold appears to be good at his job, but he doesn't care about the problems of the people who don't live in Aurora or who are affected by its need for more and more water. Because he sees no attraction in farming, he feels no compunction in bringing that way of life to an end.

4. The final quotation from Griswold shows the man's narrow view and cupidity.

5. The land is now much different from the original, natural prairie. It has been polluted with silt, salt, fertilizers, herbicides, and pesticides; that damage is hard to undo.

Sokolov, "The Dark Side of Tomatoes"

1. By devoting four paragraphs to the joys of natural tomatoes, Sokolov establishes himself as a true tomatophile. For readers with the same taste, this is a good writing decision. But readers who find tomatoes disgusting may not be engaged by this euphoric, one-sided introduction.

2. Ethylene is the same substance exuded by tomatoes to ripen themselves, so introducing an excess is not harmful or wrong.

3. Tough tomatoes are not appetizing. They are probably bought by people who also like TV dinners—their taste buds are not well developed or sensitized to natural tastes.

4. New breeds of tomatoes are developed to make them bigger and more resistant to disease.

5. Demand would have to decrease and producers would have to stop picking green tomatoes in the off-season, shipping them long distances, and trying

to ripen them in transit, before the quality of supermarket tomatoes improved.

Kaye, "Peter Jennings Gets No Self-Respect"

1. This article reveals that Jennings was a poor student who lied about a college education when he actually dropped out of school in the tenth grade. He admired his father, a news broadcaster who taught him how to describe things. His comfortable childhood left him "unchallenged, complacent," and not very well read.

2. When he was younger, he thought nothing of taking off at any time to cover a story. After three marriages, he has slowed down somewhat. When he began, he was embarrassed about his educational background and always worked to prove himself; now he is more comfortable with who he is and what he has accomplished.

3. At his best, Jennings is willing to take time to work with junior colleagues, encouraging and teaching them. At his worst, he can be devastatingly tactless. While correspondents could learn a lot from him, they could also have their confidence destroyed.

4. Kaye describes his courtships as either "madly in love or totally uninterested." Earlier accounts of his tendency to put his job before his wife, and the fact that he's been married three times, suggest that he does not generally treat his wife well. His comment to his wife that something she said was "banal" supports this view. He seems insensitive to people's feelings.

5. That Jennings wears a London Fog rather than a Burberry (which costs around $500) and buys his clothes in bulk shows that he's an ordinary guy who doesn't put on airs.

6. Jennings is more critical of himself than others are. He still bemoans his lack of education, but not as severely as he once did. Others treat him like a star, but he brushes off their compliments, can't even accept them, which suggests he doesn't feel worthy of them.

7. We don't know what he does in his spare time, if he has children, if his relationship with them parallels the relationship he had with his father, or if he ever had major problems in making his way to the top and how he overcame them. We also don't know how reliable this report is; Elizabeth Kaye is not always objective or evenhanded. She tends to include only those details that support her thesis.

Sedgwick, "The Doberman Case"

1. Information about Thor provides human interest and a frame into which the entire story fits.

2. Answers will vary. But Puppy's death shows that the vets at Angell are not always successful. Focusing on Thor alone might convey that impression.

3. They look the same, but the veterinary hospital is indestructible; in the waiting rooms, animal patients' views of each other are obstructed to avoid fights; patients in both hospitals suffer from abuse and many of the same diseases, but the animals aren't covered by insurance, so are not turned away. There are fewer vets than doctors, but vets get paid less, they work longer hours, and they are viewed as second-class doctors.

4. People usually get cats for free; cats are viewed as more self-reliant, so their medical needs are not met as often. Dogs usually must be bought and cost more than cats; they are better liked because they are more demonstrative.

5. The seal probably swallowed the coins when they were thrown at it, or into the water, at the aquarium. Obviously, people do not consider what animals will do with objects in the water or how such objects can hurt them.

6. People have pets for the same reason some people have children—for companionship and affection. People abuse pets for the same reason they abuse children—out of cruelty, stupidity, anger, and frustration. But they also abuse pets because they seem to believe that animals have no feelings and that their lives have no value.

7. Vets seem to be more motivated by love of healing than love of money. Medical doctors may not give vets the respect they deserve. See paragraphs 14–15.

8. There are relatively few hospitals for pets because costs are high and they don't receive government funding, Medicare, Medicaid, and insurance, as hospitals for people do. They must rely upon their endowment and the fees clients pay out of pocket. Hospitals are businesses, and since animal hospitals wouldn't make much money, there aren't many of them. Instead, most people take their pets to the local animal shelter or veterinary clinic, which may have from one to five doctors on staff.

Farney, "Inside Hallmark's Love Machine"

1. By "well-scrubbed," Farney means that Hallmark does not sell cards with bad language, dirty jokes, or sexual innuendos. The sample rhymes support this, as does the fact that Hallmark settled out of court and destroyed thousands of cards when accused of plagiarism, and that it is considered very bland and middle of the road by other competitors. Hallmark is unlikely to produce cards that include condoms.

2. "The more society atomizes . . . the more niches are created for greeting cards and greeting-card sales." Some new lines include divorce announcements, reconciliation cards, sympathy cards for pet owners, intimate love cards for relationships, parent-to-child cards.

3. The lyric in paragraph 15 illustrates Hallmark's well-scrubbed messages.

4. Hallmark seems like a place where old-fashioned values still exist; it would be a good place for like-minded conservatives and middle-of-the-road people to work.

5. "Engagement cards sell best in the Northeast. . . . Birthday cards saying 'Daddy' sell best in the South. . . ." This article maintains that people too busy to communicate in person buy the most cards. Also, women buy more cards than men (see paragraph 41). You might ask students why there is a gender difference.

6. Hallmark's concern with propriety, its market research, its investments into Payless Cashways and Kansas City Southern Industries illustrate that it is, indeed, a business.

7. People who respect companies that maintain ethical and traditional values, or those who send cards to people who feel this way, would probably be even more inclined to purchase from Hallmark after reading this piece. In fact, with a production of 11 million cards a day, it's probably hard to avoid buying Hallmark. Others might henceforth decide to buy cards from smaller companies.

Lemann, "Stressed Out in Suburbia"

1. The author visited Naperville "to see exactly how our familiar ideas about the suburbs have gotten out of date."

2. The population boom and real estate development, plus the move away from the big cities, led to Naperville's rapid growth. According to its master plan, it is coping well with growth to the extent that city property taxes have been lowered in the past three years.

3. People move to places like Naperville because they are new, clean, and segregated. They are relatively crime-free and filled with people who are all alike. The adults work hard so that they can make more money and be promoted, which allows them to move to an even better suburb.

4. Living in the suburbs usually means a long commute to work and a willingness to work long hours in order to afford the life-style; in between, the modern couple must take time to stay in shape and chauffeur the children to all their lessons. In the schools, there is such a competitive atmosphere that it's "painful to be average."

5. The homes are "flamboyantly traditional," with certain designs and building materials forbidden. The pseudo-European names of subdivisions reflect the social-climbing motives of the residents. Living and dining rooms have shrunk; kitchens abut a family room, but since they are open, they can't get

messy. Master bedrooms are huge; most houses also contain a small study and a large deck overlooking a fenced-in yard.

6. These authors wrote about suburbia during different periods. Lemann cites them to show how the suburbs have changed. He gives enough information about the books to help readers place them.

7. Suburban life is getting worse, with competition and resultant stress at all levels and ages.

Gould, "Women's Brains"

1. Mary Ann Evans used a man's name (George Eliot) so that she would be taken seriously and published. Eliot is considered by some critics to be one of the earliest feminists—she "well appreciated the special tragedy that biological labeling imposed upon members of disadvantaged groups." It is obvious that Gould thinks highly of her—a woman "of extraordinary talent"—and finds her representative of the best of women's brains.

2. Broca misled himself because of his belief that "women are, on the average, a little less intelligent than men." He not only failed to recognize his prejudice but also failed to take into account that women's bodies are generally smaller than men's, that the women he studied were older than the males, and that "brain weight decreases with age."

3. Since women are human beings and equal to their male counterparts, anything they/we fight for is a battle for all.

4. Gould's footnote proves that we can all be misled by our prejudices. But one miscalculation need not affect all aspects of an individual's work.

5. The quotations seem necessary to reveal the extent of early ignorance and misogyny, which led to unfounded and illogical conclusions about women. Le Bon's quotations would probably seem the most outrageous and maddening to feminist readers.

CHAPTER 7

WRITING TO EXPLAIN SOMETHING

This chapter, like Chapter 6, will be useful when the students are writing for another course. But this type of writing, in which a process is analyzed or explained, has a wide variety of applications. The essays in this chapter all involve teaching something, be it a concept or a process. To generate journal topics, have students list things they do well. In initial journal assignments, have students freewrite everything they know on each topic. These entries can then be categorized according to the types of essays in this chapter.

Have students decide which subjects could best be described by telling what it is, what it means, what it does, why it exists, or how it's done. If there are some topics that students feel unable to write about (for example, how to write well), you can give them the option of explaining why they don't do well. Reading expert Frank Smith wrote an article titled "Twelve Easy Ways to Make Reading Difficult, and One Difficult Way to Make It Easy" that could serve as a model for an explanation of how *not* to do something.

Whether they decide to use some of these journal-generated topics, one suggested by the assignments at the end of the individual readings, one of the topics provided in the notes in this manual, or one suggested at the end of the notes, you can help them develop the content by taking them through Burke's pentad of act, actor, agency, purpose, and scene. Their draft can be developed by having them freewrite on each of these elements as it relates to their topic. These freewritings should generate a good deal of material; the next step is to organize it. If the students freewrite about each element on separate sheets of paper, they can bring the papers to class, exchange them in their peer groups, and have their peers shuffle them around to determine the most logical order. Once the organization is determined, the students should be able to see which elements are the focus of the paper and which need further development.

After students have organized and developed their drafts, they can exchange them again within peer groups to get feedback on their explicitness and completeness. If students exchange with someone who knows nothing about their topic, that reader can point out gaps in the information provided. This type of feedback should help students produce a more fully developed paper.

Mona Melanson, "Beat the Butterflies"

Students should be interested in this essay, since jobs are no longer easy to find. But what else can you do with it? While this is useful information, most of them won't have such specific job interviews for at least two or three years, so you need to make it, or its format, relevant. One idea is to make it a model for a process essay. You can begin by pointing out that the author knows what she's talking about—she is a staffing consultant at Bank of America. Then ask them what topics they know about or what they know how to do well, and have them brainstorm a list. Next, ask students to tell you how Melanson's essay is organized (chronologically). You can model this process by asking the sports experts in the class to tell you how to hit a baseball. As you stand there perhaps awkwardly and ask possibly stupid questions, they will see how important it is to get steps in their proper order and to include all useful and necessary information. Following this modeling, have students freewrite a similar informational piece. If there is time left, they can read their freewriting aloud and the rest of the class can comment on the clarity and completeness of each piece.

Alan M. Dershowitz, "Shouting 'Fire!'"

In explaining why the "fire" analogy doesn't work, Dershowitz provides a useful argumentative and analytical model. After explaining the genesis of the fire analogy, he goes on to cite case after case where it has been inappropriately applied. On a personal level, your students may not be able to come up with very many similar examples. If you want to take this approach, you will probably have to provide some (for instance: "Since all freshman composition courses are offered at the same time, they are all the same," or "The Chevy Geo and the Toyota Corolla both cost the same amount, so one is as good as the other."). The students may find this technique more useful when it is applied to the writing required in other classes. To generate parallel writing tasks, you can divide them into groups of three or four, assign each group a subject (history, biology, etc.), and have them come up with one or two general questions that require this same model of explanation. When they see the relevance of this strategy, they may appreciate it more.

Norman Cousins, "Who Killed Benny Paret?"

Reaction to this essay may be mixed. The majority of students may agree that boxing is barbaric, but there will probably be a few sports fans who disagree. If that's the case, you can have each side explain (through freewriting) why boxing is or is not barbaric or who is responsible—fans, promoters, or the boxers themselves. Sharing some of these freewritings should reveal them to be fairly flat: They won't have the impact of Cousins's piece unless they include similar graphic details, and when it comes to boxing, not too many students have those at hand. So you can then go off in another direction—ask them what types of tragic situations they have personally witnessed or know of, such as the results of handgun misuse or drug abuse; then, in groups, have them develop an essay parallel to Cousins's that includes the details necessary to persuade. This sequence of tasks should make the resulting papers more persuasive and demonstrate the necessity of knowing one's subject and using specific details.

Jessica Mitford, "Embalming in the U.S.A."

This excerpt, from Mitford's *American Way of Death*, seldom fails to upset and disgust readers. So it should be fairly easy to carry on a discussion of the content. You can focus this discussion by asking students what they learned that they didn't know before; what details particularly disgusted them and why; whether, after reading this piece, they plan to have the traditional embalming and burial; and why people continue this tradition. If your focus or the eventual writing assignment will be on process, you can pair or compare this reading with Melanson's. Obviously, the only thing they have in common is their organization, but having students tell you that may enable them to see the various uses for this organizational strategy. The discussion of the specifics of embalming may be sufficient to take up the entire period. However, if you have more time, you can ask students their opinions on getting cremated. Or to illustrate cause and effect, assign a prereading freewriting on whether they'd prefer to be buried or cremated; then end the class period with a second freewriting in which they revise or expand upon the earlier one.

James P. Womack, Daniel T. Jones, and Daniel Roos, "How Lean Production Can Change the World"

This is a fairly long piece. To prepare students for it (and ensure that they read it), begin with a freewriting asking them to describe their experience with buying a car or having it repaired and to compare this experience with what Toyota advocates. During class discussion, you can go from these responses to those concerning Toyotas: Ask students who are Toyota owners how their experience corresponds to the way Toyotas are sold and serviced in Japan. This should lead to a focus on why American auto plants cannot, or do not, change their outdated sales and production methods. The main points of this entire discussion should be put on the board, since they serve as models for comparison-contrast and cause-effect organization, while also demonstrating the analytical process.

Pat Mora, "A Letter to Gabriela, a Young Writer"

It would be interesting to pair this essay with the piece by Richard Rodriguez or the one by Barbara Mellix and have students write about the similarities regarding race, reading, and writing—what the authors have learned about life and how much of this may have come from writing. Follow up by asking students what they have learned from writing. A general question will probably not elicit many answers or involve the majority of the class; instead, ask them to freewrite about "a time when you learned something about yourself, or life, as a result of writing." If you make the topic personally relevant, they should be able to understand the significance of Mora's letter. If this approach is a success, you may want to consider asking students to compose a letter about writing to someone they want to encourage (perhaps high school seniors or prospective college freshmen).

Flannery O'Connor, "The Nature and Aim of Fiction"

This essay can be paired with Mora's to expand the discussion of writing. You could also add William Stafford's "Why I Write" to show that a man's perspective is no different. Then ask students to explain why these authors write and respect writing, or ask why they (the students) do or do not consider themselves to be writers. Examining the answers to these freewritings should lead to a good discussion. Once a definition of good writers has been established, you might move on to an examination of what constitutes good writing. O'Connor notes that "these are times when the financial rewards for sorry writing are much greater than those for good writing. There are certain cases in which, if you can only learn to write poorly enough, you can make a great deal of money." Stephen King is a good example to bring up here. Stylistically, he's awful, yet he's very effective. If you begin a discussion of good versus successful writers with King, you can proceed by asking students who they consider good and why. A good way to illustrate the difference is to assign O'Connor along with a short story by King and one by Henry James or another master, either past or present, or one from Chapter 10. Then have students apply O'Connor's criteria for art and successful writing to these stories. Clearly, this is a long assignment that will take more than one class period, but it might be worth it, especially as you prepare to move on to the next chapter.

ADDITIONAL WRITING ASSIGNMENTS

1. *Business.* Cousins, Mitford, and Womack, Jones, and Roos explain how various businesses operate. Cousins looks at boxing, Mitford at funerals, and the Womack team at the auto industry. The first two pieces are critical, while the third is more analytical. If a certain field appeals to you, decide on your focus and purpose and then set out to conduct some research. You may need to interview people on the job and/or look for information in business journals. After you have collected sufficient information, you may want to model your organization on one of these authors, although form usually follows function. That is, decide on your purpose and form should follow.

2. *Activities.* Melanson, Mitford, Mora, and Womack, Jones, and Roos write about various activities—how to prepare for an interview, how to prepare a dead body, how to become a writer, how the auto industry works. They write on these topics for a reason, either to give advice or to give warnings. Whatever their purpose, they write because they know what they're talking about. If you have expertise on a subject and feel that others would profit from reading about it, you may want to take this approach. To decide on a topic, make a list of things you are good at; then narrow it to one topic worth writing about. Model your paper on one of the authors mentioned above.

3. *On writing*. Mora and O'Connor discuss what it takes to be a writer and to write well. Mora focuses primarily on personal experience and the role her heritage plays. O'Connor takes a more traditional approach: She gives her opinion and then backs it up and exemplifies it with examples from the masters. If you are interested in writing, you may want to develop this topic, emulating either of these authors' approaches or creating your own. Tell about what makes you a writer—why writing is important to you, why you like it, or who influenced your attitudes and development.

ANSWERS TO QUESTIONS

Melanson, "Beat the Butterflies"

1. Agreement with Melanson depends upon one's definition of "first job." For many students, a first job comes long before college graduation, and that job may indeed be extremely important, because it teaches responsibility and reinforces all those lessons the student has been taught by parents and teachers in a real-world context. Yet even if students have had other nonprofessional jobs, the first "real" one will be important, for it is their first chance to prove themselves as professionals.

2. Asking questions lets the interviewer know that you have some knowledge about and interest in the company, that you know enough to ask the right questions, and that you are articulate. It also lets applicants know whether the job is right for them.

3. Advising applicants to write an immediate thank-you letter is a tip I had never heard before in this context. Writing an evaluative note to oneself is also a new tip.

4. Melanson offers no guarantees except that this preparation will make the applicant less nervous.

5. The steps in this piece are arranged chronologically, which should help the applicant prepare. Labeling them as steps makes them easier to separate and prepare for.

Dershowitz, "Shouting 'Fire!'"

1. Holmes wrote his decision during the beginning of World War I; it involved a case in which two socialists had been inciting draftees to resist.

2. The Schenck case involved a pamphlet that asked readers to think about the message and then decide whether to resist; the fire analogy is not political and does not ask listeners to think but to act without thinking. The analogy is insulting because "most Americans do not respond to political rhetoric with the same kind of automatic acceptance expected of schoolchildren responding to a fire drill."

3. By including *falsely,* the analogy implies that unnecessary panic would be caused. The implication of the sentence is that he would approve the shout if it were true. Given his stance and ruling on the Schenck case, Holmes probably would not support the right to mistakenly shout "Fire!"

4. The government should prosecute speech that threatens individual safety or government security and may even be correct in punishing obscenity and libelous speech.

5. Comparing the reactions of schoolchildren to a fire alarm with adults' reaction in a crowded theater stretches the analogy a bit.

6. Dershowitz cites a number of cases in which the analogy was misapplied; he also points out that "analogies are, by their nature, matters of degree. Some are closer to the core example than others."

Cousins, "Who Killed Benny Paret?"

1. This conversation puts the situation into context; Cousins cites an authority on boxing whose statements exemplify what Cousins wants to attack. Jacobs's view shows why Benny Paret was killed. Cousins may have cited the date of the conversation precisely to imply that this view *is* dated, yet boxing is still big business, or to show that the problem is long-standing.

2. The transitional paragraph provides a good illustration of what happens when people support this type of activity. It also has a shock value; it hits the reader in the face with the results of boxing.

3. Investigators questioned the wisdom of the referees, the doctors who had declared Paret fit to fight, and Paret's manager. Cousins believes they overlooked the real cause—a blow to the head.

4. Including all these details, in sequence, shows exactly what happens when a man is hit this hard. The sentence flows because all its parts are parallel—when, when, when.

5. Cousins explains the details leading up to Paret's death to show the barbarity of boxing. This type of explanation is known as an indirect argument—its details appeal to the readers' emotions.

6. Fighting has changed somewhat, as evidenced on March 8, 1990, when referee Richard Steele stopped the heavyweight fight between Mike Tyson and Donovan "Razor" Ruddock at 2 minutes 22 seconds of the seventh round, because he felt Ruddock had had enough. Steele said he stopped it because "I could see in his face that surrendering look. He didn't want no more. . . . When he went back his balance was gone. He was helpless." But referee Steele is in the minority; the boxing crowd was outraged. As Steele said, "People want to see somebody prone" (*St. Louis Post-Dispatch,* 27 June 1991: 7D).

Mitford, "Embalming in the U.S.Å."

1. Embalming used to be done in the deceased's home, so it was almost like keeping a wake, a sign of respect, to observe the process. I cannot believe that anyone, except perhaps budding morticians, would want to witness this process.

2. *Demisurgeon* means, literally, half-surgeon. However, morticians use it interchangeably with *dermasurgeon*. The former may be more appropriate since morticians lack the skill and training of a true surgeon.

3. By giving the object of embalming a name, Mitford reminds the reader that this is a human being. Jones is such a common name that it represents Everyman.

4. Mitford's use of French terms parodies the funeral industry's use of supposedly acceptable euphemisms to elevate its craft. She makes fun of the language by reproducing its cutesy spellings, such as "Lyf-Lyk tint." At the same time, she is indirectly poking fun at the beauty business. Her extremely precise descriptions are more than enough to make the process gruesome and unattractive.

5. The custom persists in part because it is a custom but also because people are totally unaware of what embalming and preparing the body for viewing consists of. If more people knew what went on, the funeral business would quickly decline—which is probably why people are "dissuaded" from observing the embalming process.

Womack, Jones, and Roos, "How Lean Production Can Change the World"

1. The authors found that the best American plants in the United States are "now more productive than the average Japanese auto plant—and are very nearly equal in quality."

2. The dealers are under contract only to that company, and they have to pay for their cars upon receipt, which means that the plant's assembly lines can keep going while the dealers wait for sales. Also, the dealers have to buy what the plant sells them.

3. In Japan, dealers sell from door to door. They precede their sales by doing demographic studies, so they know who the best customers are; during sales visits, they take in more data, which goes to the plant, so cars can be made to accommodate buyers' needs. This system gives the customer the advantage of personal and long-term service; the disadvantage is that it is hard to escape this relationship. For the dealers, the latter is a mixed blessing. They are ensured customers, but the approach is costly.

4. The Japanese government has strict import duties, which makes non-Japanese cars prohibitively expensive.

5. The amount of time and detail devoted to the history of mass production shows its uniquely American character, which helps to explain why the industry has been reluctant to make large changes. The focus would have been stronger without all this detail, but the resistance might have been less understandable. The organization works to show the contrast between American and Japanese methods.

6. Mass production was successful for so long because it made American cars affordable. However, the size of these plants made the process impersonal, which began to result in lower-quality products. In contrast, Japanese workers have a personal stake in their companies and production, so they produce better-quality products. This has also resulted in greater efficiency and productivity—and hence lower prices.

7. Mass production companies rely on in-house suppliers for almost 70 percent of their needs; lean production companies for only 27 percent. Nevertheless, the Japanese developed better relationships with their suppliers, which led to higher quality and better prices for parts, since there is less competition and secrecy. The result is lower-cost cars.

8. To shift to lean production methods, American car companies will have to change their "ideas about work" and then sell this concept to union management, which will in turn have to convince the workers. None of this will be easy, owing to the long history of mass production and hierarchical organization. But the shift is necessary and worth the trouble; without it, American car companies will go out of business.

Mora, "A Letter to Gabriela, a Young Writer"

1. The letter format makes the approach more personal, which makes sense in this context, since part of the content deals with Mora's and Gabriela's common heritage. The examples Mora uses as an alternative to writing in the first paragraph establish who her primary reader is. Yet her message is clearly directed at a wider audience because of its wider implications about writing and society.

2. Mora writes because she is a reader, because she wants to communicate with people she has never met, because writing enables her to develop her thoughts better than speaking does, because writing is a private endeavor, because she's curious, and because Mexican Americans need "to be published and to be studied in schools and colleges" so that their stories and ideas won't disappear, so that they will gain some respect. All of these are important; as a white Anglo educator, the general reasons are more important to me and my teaching, while the specific, heritage-related reasons seem more important to Mora.

3. These admissions lead one to realize that all people are alike and that no one is better than anyone else.

4. The only way to improve is to take risks, to experiment; initially, these experiments will not work out. But one learns through trial and error.

5. The analogy makes sense to writers, though it is not always evident to inexperienced writers, who believe that good writers get it right the first time and that they are born, not made.

6. Writers have to keep some objectivity about their work so that they will be willing and able to revise, to listen to others, and to use constructive criticism.

O'Connor, "The Nature and Aim of Fiction"

1. Many people view writers as different, almost freaks, since they believe writing is very difficult and good writing almost unattainable.

2. O'Connor wants people to understand that there are many types of writers and many ways to go about writing. It is not a magical process available to only a chosen few.

3. As O'Connor notes, some writers are in the business only to make money and make it quickly. Laboring over a work means waiting a longer period of time until one gets paid. Moreover, much of the public does not value good writing, so some writers see no need to aim for it. Instead, they aim to appeal to the public's tastes.

4. Writers have "the habit of art," of "writing something that is valuable in itself and that works in itself." Symbols "operate in depth as well as on the surface, increasing the story in every direction." Writers need a vision that "is able to see different levels of reality in one image or one situation."

5. These sentences illustrate Flaubert's skill, care, and art.

6. Modern fiction does not seem to include traces of the author. "The reader is on his own, floundering around in the thoughts of various unsavory characters. He finds himself in the middle of a world apparently without comment." O'Connor believes it takes different dispositions to write novels and short stories. While both are stories, writing a novel involves more hope, pain, and energy.

7. She believes people should read anything and everything.

8. On one level, practically everything O'Connor says about writing fiction can apply to nonfiction, if the writer is good. But one has to define *nonfiction*. Some nonfiction, such as technical manuals, seldom requires or includes symbol or vision.

9. Writing teachers can teach their students "the limits and possibilities of words and the respect due them." They cannot "put the gift" into their students, but they can "try to keep it from going in an obviously wrong direction." Students can also benefit from teachers who serve as coaches, who can show them new strategies for developing their writing.

CHAPTER 8

WRITING TO EVALUATE SOMETHING

Although evaluation is something we all do every day, students often have difficulty when they have to do it in writing. They tend to summarize or describe rather than evaluate. The main problem usually lies in the inability to define and isolate criteria for analysis; a secondary problem arises when students have to evaluate something they know little about. Some modeling and prewriting work can help alleviate both of these problems.

Perhaps two of the most familiar modes of evaluation are restaurant and movie reviews. Yet movie reviews are often flawed because students do not have highly developed criteria for evaluation—they like the story, or the action, or the main character, but they don't know why or what to say about it without summarizing the movie (a bad habit movie reviewers also fall into). So you may want to discourage movie reviews as a model or potential paper topic. Restaurant evaluations are somewhat better models, since they embody clear criteria—quality and variety of food, service, ambiance, price, location, and so forth. If you want to model the task of evaluation, you can tell the class that you are going to prepare a restaurant guide for new students on campus and ask them to develop criteria, assign groups to visit each site, pool their evaluations, and write the reviews. This type of task introduces some fun into the assignment while also providing a model for developing an evaluative paper.

When you feel that students understand how to develop criteria, you will need to help them select a paper topic. As always, the Suggestions for Writing in the text offer specific topics based on the essays; the Additional Writing Assignments in this manual synthesize the essays into three general topoi: pop culture, art and literature, and historical (or famous) figures. If the choice for evaluation is wide open, students can refer to earlier journal entries on what they do well and are interested in. If you prefer that they restrict their topics to the three general areas, you can follow the formula prescribed in an earlier chapter: Under each heading (pop culture, etc.), have them list people or issues they are interested in. When this list is compiled, have them narrow it by marking those areas they also know something about. Then they can choose one to three topoi for freewriting to see which they know the most about.

After topics have been chosen, you will need to work with students in developing criteria. Have students announce their topics so that you can list them on the board; then group people according to similar topics. Within each group, students can then develop their own criteria for evaluation. You may want to provide initial guidance by giving some general headings, such as the item's or issue's nature, quality, importance, benefit, and value or worth. If these headings don't help, you can have them use the elements of the pentad—act, actor, agency, scene, purpose—to decide upon criteria. As the students develop their criteria, they can divide their findings into those that can be developed through knowledge and experience and those that will need to be evaluated on the basis of research; and they can decide whether these criteria are established on the basis of external or internal judgments.

The next step is to send them out to gather research or conduct observations. When all the data have been gathered, you can provide a focus for the evaluation by having students do a freewriting that provides background information on the topic. On the basis of this paragraph, they may be able to decide how they want to organize the body of the paper—by using strengths and weaknesses or by using one or more of the traditional modes: cause-effect, comparison-contrast, narrative, historical or chronological approach. If they aren't sure which approach would work best, refer students to the essays in this chapter. Have them do a rough topic outline of the essay that appears to parallel their topic and then fill in the blanks with their own information.

These strategies should provide some initial guidance. But students won't know what really works until they write their first draft and get some feedback from their group members. Since students are grouped according to similar topics, reading each other's papers may provide the most effective guidance.

Ruth Dorgan, "Jack the Giantmugger"

Since practically every student is familiar with this fairy tale, they should enjoy Dorgan's analysis. In fact, her approach may take away the mystery surrounding the idea of evaluating or analyzing literature or any written prose. To introduce the concept of evaluation, have students determine the main focus for her evaluation (Jack's character) and list the different elements she critiques. Once the criteria for evaluation are clear, ask students to think of other fairy tales in which the hero or heroine is undeserving. Then assign a fairy tale per small group and have them do a character analysis like Dorgan's. This type of exercise should help students assimilate one aspect of evaluation, which can later be applied to a longer, more serious piece of prose.

Nora Ephron, "*People* Magazine"

Dorgan and Ephron use basically the same mode of evaluation: They discuss the things they don't like. That should be an easy method to remember. But students may not agree with this piece. In fact, one way to open discussion is to have them take the opposite stance: Evaluate *People* on the basis of what they do like. This approach gets them involved in a key element of evaluation— taking the topic apart to find criteria to support the thesis. Of course, evaluation is a little more involved than that. As Ephron's piece illustrates, a successful evaluation is also based on the critic's knowledge of the genre and comparison with (in this case) a better example or exemplar. Thus, for the students' evaluations to be successful, they need to be informed readers of similar but perhaps lesser magazines, such as the *Star* or *National Enquirer,* so that their evaluation is supported by comparing *People's* qualities with the qualities of one of those supermarket tabloids. Clearly, we are not attacking great literature; nevertheless, the methods of evaluation are similar, no matter what the genre.

Luc Sante, "Unlike a Virgin"

Students should love this essay. Since Madonna appeals primarily to teenage girls, your students will have the advantage of having experienced her appeal and also, perhaps, of having outgrown it, so they can knowledgeably judge this essay. Like the authors of preceding pieces in this chapter, Sante relies on background information and a comparison within similar contexts to evaluate Madonna. Unlike the others, he moves chronologically. As he traces Madonna's career, he does not explicitly condemn or criticize; he compares. In the process, she emerges as "a bad actress, a barely adequate singer, a graceless dancer, a boring interview subject, a workmanlike but uninspired (co-)songwriter, and a dynamo of hard work and ferocious ambition." But Sante saves this explicit judgment until the very end. Up until that point, he appears objective, merely pointing out, through comparisons, how unoriginal her work has been. To demonstrate his strategy, you can divide the students into groups, assign one page per group, and have each group analyze the criteria used to judge Madonna. The chronology should be fairly clear, since the students are familiar with it. The references to similar work by earlier performers may not be familiar but should emerge in each stage of her career. Tracing Sante's method of analysis as it applies to a familiar topic should enable students to apply it in a larger assignment.

R. Jackson Wilson, "A Man Watching"

This short piece is a model of evaluating art as a symbol. Since the picture is included with the essay, students can judge how well Wilson describes it and its effect. Since you're dealing with underclassmen, your students probably will not appreciate the relationship of the picture to Whitman's persona or to *Leaves of Grass*. The introduction to Whitman in *American Literature*, Book B (Brooks, Lewis, and Warren, eds.), provides some excellent background information on Whitman himself; Sections 8, 11, and 32 of *Leaves* are good examples of his "watching" imagery and illustrate why the picture is so appropriate. Wilson's method of evaluation is similar to that of others in this chapter in that he uses comparison, taking apart elements of the picture and comparing their effect to Whitman's purpose and persona. You can have students apply this method by asking them to bring in their favorite album and describe how the cover symbolizes or represents the content/lyrics. This method will be clearer if you model it first; but for modeling to be effective, you will need to provide liner notes and/or play some of the album before you launch into your own comparative analysis. While this strategy may seem to be steeped in pop culture, this method of analysis is one students can use in other classes, such as art history.

Bruce Catton, "Grant and Lee"

Like other authors in this chapter, Catton uses contrast as a basis for evaluation. However, he differs from the others in his conclusion, which shows that differing backgrounds can have positive effects: Each can yield equally fine men. This is not necessarily a novel thesis; however, within the focus of a single context (the Civil War), it makes a point. How can students learn from this model? Obviously, it needs to be put into a relevant context. For example, have them focus on a familiar unit—the family. They can analyze the success of their parents by tracing their diverse backgrounds and showing how they interact to produce a united front and, by extension, successful children. Once this pattern is modeled, ask the class to brainstorm other contexts in which two differing characters combine for positive effect (buddy movies come to mind, although political scenarios and historical figures will put this exercise on a higher plane). The key here, as with the other assignments, is to make the evaluative techniques clear so that they can be applied in the students' own writing, in this class or in others.

Mark Twain, "Fenimore Cooper's Literary Offenses"

Most students will be familiar with Twain, though not all will have read or heard of Cooper. Twain's reputation and tone should get them involved in the essay, and his examples preclude the need (or desire) to read Cooper. At first, his list of "rules governing literary art" seem a little vague, but as he continues, his examples clarify what he means. His next-to-last paragraph is more specific and may provide a more useful model for your students to follow in similarly evaluating a literary work. You can have them apply his guidelines to one of the short stories in Chapter 10; you can model this approach by asking students to provide examples for evaluation. Television shows, popular novels, and movies are familiar contexts, although many students may have read the same best-selling novel. Once a model has been decided upon, evaluate it as a class or within small groups. Either of these strategies should enable students to apply this evaluative approach to more substantive works.

Dorothy Rabinowitz, "From the Mouths of Babes to a Jail Cell"

Despite its length, most students should find this study interesting to read. Before they read, though, have them freewrite on child abuse. Then you can begin class (after they have read the essay) by asking whether this piece has made them reconsider their views. To bring out its evaluative techniques and also reveal your students' level of belief or bias, you can ask them them to freewrite or debate whether or not they believe Rabinowitz's conclusion—that these cases of alleged child abuse are only the result of hysteria in a society "afflicted by some paroxysm of virtue" similar to that of the Salem witch-hunts and McCarthy trials—and on what they base their beliefs. If they have read the piece closely, the amount of evidence should be persuasive; however, you may find some, like those involved with the Kelly Michaels case, who simply refuse to believe the children could be making up their stories. Such disparate opinions should result in a good discussion, whose points of evidence should be noted on the board. This resulting list provides yet another model for evaluation—a compilation of facts based on research and interviews.

ADDITIONAL WRITING ASSIGNMENTS

1. *Pop culture and society.* Ephron, Sante, and Rabinowitz each evaluate an element of current society—a magazine, a pop idol, a national hysteria. Each author does so to make a point, to show through comparison the error in current evaluations. Ehpron compares *People* magazine with *Life;* Sante compares Madonna with other show business figures; Rabinowitz compares the Michaels trial with witch-hunts. Choose an issue or figure you feel has been greatly overrated or misjudged; base your selection on a knowledge of that area or a willingness to back up your thesis with research. Then decide on the reasons for your thesis—the criteria for evaluation. Develop your evaluation through comparison.

2. *Art and literature.* Wilson, Dorgan, and Twain have a similar focus but have differing purposes and employ different techniques for evaluation. Wilson shows how art can symbolize an author or work of literature; Twain and Dorgan show how an author or character has been overrated. If you have knowledge and interest in art or literature, decide upon a focus and purpose for evaluation; then determine your criteria and write your essay.

3. *Historical figures.* Catton and Rabinowitz trace the background of their subjects to evaluate their success or failure. In the process, they also employ comparison and use relevant context to prove their points. This type of evaluation relies on research, using both primary and secondary sources. As you begin your research, be sure to include not only pertinent facts about your topic but also elements for comparison. Then write your evaluation on the basis of your research.

ANSWERS TO QUESTIONS

Dorgan, "Jack the Giantmugger"

1. Dorgan's thesis comes in the middle of paragraph 1. Her evidence is a summary of the story: "Jack is a shiftless, irresponsible wastrel who turns to thieving when he has ruined his poor mother and himself," plus examples from the text itself.

2. In this society, being different means not being average, not "fitting in." Just as fairy tales are analogous to life, so too is Dorgan's point.

3. Whether these attitudes seem recognizable will depend on the individual's experiences, either at home or in society. Even if children have nonchauvinistic parents, they will still encounter such models on television and in the movies.

4. To Dorgan, Jack represents the stereotypical narrow-minded, chauvinistic male, a thief who will steal your pride and your possessions. Her closing line suggests he represents a large class of people. Jack can't do anything to

please Dorgan; she criticizes his every act, beginning with trading the cow for the beans.

5. Dorgan likes the giant, calling him "at heart solitary and esthetic . . . a lover of beauty, . . . [an owner of] beautiful things." She concedes that he is a male chauvinist, but she points out that this is a common fault. As for his roaring, she notes that this is natural for giants but implies that it need not be cause for alarm.

Ephron, *"People* Magazine"

1. *People* makes Ephron grouchy because it's intellectual junk food; she feels lousy after she reads it. What makes her feel worst is that the magazine appeals to a lot of people, who accept its low-brow mediocrity.

2. The magazine was developed around "a simple, five-word idea: let's-call-a-magazine *People*." Ephron attributes it to Kierkegaard, who said "in time, all anyone would be interested in was gossip." Since most newsstands are now in supermarkets, the editors felt the magazine should appeal to women.

3. In her introduction, Ehpron admits that she reads the magazine—even buys it—and reads it all the way through. In paragraph 8, she tries to be fair, beginning each comparison with something like "I have nothing against . . ." then following with a big "but."

4. Ephron defines *celebrity* as "anyone I would stand up in a restaurant and stare at," but she feels *People* has changed that definition so that *celebrity* is "anyone *People* writes about." Such status is probably not lasting. As Andy Warhol said, everyone has their fifteen minutes. Who is familiar will depend upon the age, education, and experience of the reader.

5. Ephron comes across as a lover of good literature and quality journalism. She obviously does not relate to the nonreaders who buy "mass-market women's magazines." She wants a magazine that "delivers the goods."

Sante, "Unlike a Virgin"

1. Madonna became famous because of her hard work and ambition, which Sante cites as two positive attributes. She has risen because she has been "brilliant at imposing herself on the attention of the world" and because she can change her "shape" to fit the public's needs.

2. Madonna's role models are David Bowie and Marilyn Monroe.

3. She appeals primarily to teenage girls who "admire her as a workhorse and a career strategist (and because she scares teenage boys)." This essay is not written for teenage girls; it takes a less-than-adoring look at their idol.

4. In paragraph 25, Sante sums up his objections: "Madonna, then, is a bad actress, a barely adequate singer, a graceless dancer, a boring interview

subject, a workmanlike but uninspired (co-)songwriter. . . . Her pool of ideas . . . . is limited. . . . Her ability to titillate will wane with time."

5.   Madonna is a pop sensation who lacks the talent to endure. If she wants to stay in show business, she will have to keep on top of the most current trends, which "requires speed and fluidity of humans, and in ever-increasing amounts."

Wilson, "A Man Watching"

1.   The fact that this picture is made from a daguerreotype seems in keeping with Whitman's age and time. This origin adds legitimacy to the evaluation since the picture is an evaluation of Whitman.

2.   Wilson explains that the size "was necessary because engraving needed to be condensed enough so that the lines and hatchings did not show too plainly." Putting the picture on a larger blank page heightens the "effect of solitude and separation."

3.   As some of Whitman's poetry demonstrates, he had a habit of sitting apart and observing. This is different from an occasional glance.

4.   What is visible in the picture suggests a man whose poetry would not be rigid or formal and would therefore be different from the other poetry of the period (or any that had come before him).

Catton, "Grant and Lee"

1.   Each general represented the side he defended—Grant was a man of the North, while Lee personified the South.

2.   Catton presents a fairly objective portrait; he is neither sympathetic nor critical. His conclusion praises them both.

3.   The setting lent privacy and dignity to the proceedings and allowed the men to work out the peace without worrying about its effects on an audience. A domestic scene is appropriate for healing. A meeting at Grant's headquarters or at the White House would have humiliated the South. A meeting on the battlefield would have suggested that the war wasn't really over.

4.   The essay would have been much shorter if similarities were compared. Catton's point is made stronger by showing how such different men came to agree.

5.   Catton's organization works well. He deals equally with each man's differing personality in order to lead the reader into the conclusion, which builds on their similarities.

Twain, "Fenimore Cooper's Literary Offenses"

1. Twain uses these quotations to stand in opposition to his thesis. By refuting the theories of authorities, Twain's own becomes much stronger than if he were arguing with illiterates.

2. Each rule builds on the premise established in the previous one. His rules about consistency seem like some of the most important to follow, in fiction and nonfiction. In comparison with the previous eleven, the last seven, dealing with grammar and diction, are of less importance.

3. Writers need to be good observers so that their writing is realistic. Because many of Cooper's descriptions are vague, coincidental, or unrealistic, Twain believes he was not a good observer. Twain persuades the reader of this by citing passages and examples from Cooper's novels.

4. Calling a woman a female tends to dehumanize her.

5. Twain shifts his diction when he exaggerates the idiomatic expression "a grain of salt" to make his point humorously and emphatically.

6. Cooper's dialogue is awkward, stiff, lacking purpose, irrelevant, off the subject, uninteresting, unrelated to the plot, and excessive. Twain's examples support some of these charges.

7. Dead writers are usually attacked by living writers who feel the former do not deserve their reputation. Writers making such attacks will often be pleased to see the public give them the praise formerly directed toward others.

Rabinowitz, "From the Mouths of Babes to a Jail Cell"

1. There were 131 counts of sexual abuse made against Michaels. Rabinowitz writes about this because she believes they are implausible. Her case is well supported.

2. Rabinowitz wrote about this case because she believed it was a huge miscarriage of justice, made possible by society's hysteria about child abuse, and because she was outraged by her profession's failure to go against public opinion and research the facts. She goes into detail to prove just how the case was mishandled. Given the growing number of child abuse cases, the Michaels case has grave national implications.

3. The analogy is based upon the fact that both proceeded because of society's acceptance of "trial by accusation." They differ because Rabinowitz had mountains of research to substantiate Michaels's innocence, because the accusers are children, and because child abuse suspects have been tried in the media.

4. The problem with this motto is that the children were very often intimidated, led, and told what to say. If the children's stories had been believed, these trials would not have occurred. The prosecutors believed the stories the children were told to tell.

5. The 1979 Federal Child Abuse Act "dramatically increased funds available to states and localities for such agencies and experts."

6. Michaels's attorneys believed she was innocent and that merely pointing out the problems with logistics would be enough to prove it. Given the public's and prosecutor's tendency to ignore anything they didn't want to hear, character witnesses probably would not have helped.

7. Fonolleras went into the case convinced that Michaels was guilty. He was also unprofessional, failing to tape-record interviews and destroying his notes. He was a scandalmonger.

8. Kelly Michaels's trial was a travesty of justice.

CHAPTER 9

WRITING TO EXPLORE AN IDEA

With this chapter, students return to what some may see as "fun" writing. If they choose a creative, exploratory stance, their writing will be much less structured than what they've done in the previous two chapters. Even if they decide to write a critical piece, the preliminary writing will be fairly creative and unstructured as they decide what they think and want to say. But while creativity can be attractive, it also has certain risks. Lack of structure can turn into lack of unity and coherence if students think writing to explore means that they are free to write a series of unconnected generalizations. Compared with the eight motives discussed in previous chapters, writing to explore may give writers the most freedom, yet freedom can be bewildering to inexperienced writers who like a clear sense of "what the teacher wants"—hence the decision to locate this chapter toward the end of the book.

What should they write on? The readings in this chapter examine the general themes of racial and cultural differences and an analysis of animal behavior. The notes in this manual for the readings include suggestions for developing each of these topics, but if students find them unstimulating, you'll have to come up with something else. Probably everyone is curious about something: Why have Nazi philosophies become increasingly popular? Why did the American public accept Ronald Reagan? Why don't people care about the diminishing ozone layer? Why don't American automakers start competing with the Japanese? Why are women attracted to thoughtless men? The list could go on and on, but students may need some prompting.

Use these questions, or some of your own, as prompts. List them on the board. Then ask students to make their own list. Give them five to ten minutes and a minimum length, maybe five to ten questions. When they have finished, have students share their questions. You can cut down on repetition if you have them compare their lists in small groups first and compile a master list, so that each question is only asked once. These questions should then be listed on the board to stimulate further ideas.

Once a master list has been compiled, have students write down their own lists as ideas for journal entries for this chapter. According to their interests and knowledge, they can either make a list of the top five questions they'd like to explore or make two lists—one of items they will explore and one of problems they will attempt to solve. The first list calls for creative thinking and the second list, being more critical, calls for analysis. Since we all have differing interests and strengths, students should have the option of deciding which type of thinking they wish to pursue.

Whatever direction students take, the first step will be the same: Explore what they know and speculate on reasons for this problem. This type of writing assignment should be done for each topic they plan to explore, so that the less intriguing problems eventually can be discarded.

When students have narrowed their focus to a single area for exploration, they will be ready for the next step: gathering information. If their topic involves the immediate environment, they can use their journals to take field notes and to observe behaviors as part of the information-gathering process. Observation may also be extended to interviews. Depending upon the topic, students may want to poll subjects for their views. If the topic is not immediately accessible, students will need to use the library to gather information. You may also want to allow students working on the same topic to share information. This approach will broaden their findings but probably will not influence their conclusions, which will depend upon the individual student's interpretations of the information.

Obviously, this project can be as large as you want to make it. But at some point, the information gathering will have to cease and students must begin to analyze and synthesize their findings. To help students focus their themes, direct them back to their initial freewritings in which they raised questions about their topic. If, for example, a student has explored the question of why there has been a rise of racial intolerance and hate groups in recent years, he may find that there are a number of reasons. In analyzing them, he may notice that they are all related to a single factor, which can lead him to draw his conclusions. On the other hand, if a student has explored the question of why people are cruel to animals, she may have come up with a number of answers but discovered that they can be classified according to age, sex, or background. These findings may lead her to offer suggestions for resolving the problem.

This element of the exploratory process will be the most difficult for students; not many are accustomed to the freedom of thinking critically and drawing conclusions—at least not in academia. To help them synthesize their material, you may also want to direct students to the readings and have them extrapolate the procedures the authors used to deal with their findings.

When you feel that students have adequately analyzed their material, lead a discussion on how they should proceed with their writing. You may wish to focus on organization and appeal to an audience. Again, you can refer them to the readings for strategies. In the readings they may discover that narration is a useful way to engage the reader or to make a subtle point. To see the value of this strategy, have students write a narration about some part of their topic—a background story about why they became interested in the subject, an anecdote detailing their observation of a typical subject, a synthesis of the entire topic into one succinct analogy, or a hypothetical scene developed as a result of the student's conclusions. Sharing these narratives with their peers will reveal the variety of uses for narration and may stimulate ideas for developing parts of their paper, such as the introduction or the conclusion, or their entire essay.

When the drafts have reached a reasonable stage of development, you may want to refer students to the text one last time. Have them analyze the different ways the authors concluded their explorations. No matter how the students' exploratory essays were developed, they should be able to find an appropriate model for concluding their papers.

Jane Goodall, "The Mind of the Chimpanzee"

This is a fascinating piece, one that students should enjoy. To ensure that they read it, and to start a discussion, ask them to freewrite a response, either open-ended or focused, telling you what they learned from reading the essay. An open-ended assignment will yield a greater variety of responses, ranging from feelings about the scientific community to reactions against animal experimentation; a focused assignment will lead to a more uniform discussion. The type of assignment you use depends on what you want to do with it. The open-ended response can be the basis for a longer paper based on the ideas elicited; the focused response can be used as a model for a similar paper: "Tell about a time when you learned something from observing an animal's behavior; how did it resemble humans'?" Whatever direction the written responses and follow-up assignments take, you may wish to spend the remainder of class time having students analyze Goodall's organization so that they have a model for developing their own papers.

James Fallows, "Land of Plenty"

At first reading, the custom Fallows describes in this piece may seem completely at odds with some of our American customs; indeed, Fallows makes this point fairly clear, even though he also is comparing *sodai gomi* to Malaysian customs. But if you've ever driven around on trash night, you know that Americans, too, throw away perfectly good items—yet we are castigated as wasteful and frivolous, while the Japanese have the reputation of being responsible and thrifty. In other words, both cultures have inaccurate reputations, but only ours is negative. To see whether this irony is obvious to students, ask them to respond to the essay by comparing this Japanese custom with America's. Once the similarities have been noted, discussion can continue by focusing on American customs that might seem odd to foreigners. Or if your class contains any seasoned travelers, you may wish to explore other foreign customs that appear to differ from ours but that may have some undiscerned parallels. If time remains, you can focus these findings by discussing Fallows's use of narrative to reveal these differences and its effect on the students as readers. This discussion will remind or reveal to them another strategy to use in writing to explore an idea.

Gloria Naylor, "Mommy, What Does 'Nigger' Mean?"

Like Fallows, Naylor uses narrative to explain the effects of cultural (and intercultural) behavior. Like Goodall's piece, this one may also include information the students were previously unaware of. Nevertheless, if you have black students in your class, it may be difficult to get a discussion going. No matter what level of prejudice exists, there is always a fear of offending or hurting another's feelings in that context. You may be able to overcome this problem by having students freewrite a response to the question "How did this essay make you feel?" Their freewritings will probably reveal similar feelings and can also lead naturally into a discussion of the effect of the narrative introduction on eliciting these feelings. This can lead to a closer examination of the essay's overall structure—introduction, narrative, explanation-examples comparing black and white usage, and conclusion. Once this pattern is clear, ask students to discuss epithets—social, cultural, or personal denigration—that have hurt them. Are there similar linguistic and intercultural distinctions (whitey, Jew, hillbilly, shorty)? If there are, the discussion should lead to some understanding of what blacks have to endure; if there are not, students may be ready at this point to look at the reasons for these different usages and their effects.

Richard Selzer, "How to Build a Slaughterhouse"

An interesting way to begin a discussion of this piece is to ask the class, "How many of you got past the reality of the slaughterhouse to Selzer's idealization?" Could any of them read the essay and then, like Selzer, coolly eat a hamburger for lunch? In this age of gang wars, famine, and graphically violent movies, does this description move them? Or do they find the slaughterhouse section more engaging to read than Selzer's paragraphs about the site of "mythic imagination"?

Or you may wish to take another approach. When assigning this piece, you can advise students that it changes midway through: "Don't get discouraged if you find the first half of this essay upsetting. It changes; keep reading." It may also be helpful to provide some background information on why Selzer set up his idealistic scene by referring to some classic biblical or mythical scenes.

In class, assign a two-part freewriting question, asking students what they liked or disliked about the essay, followed by a question asking them to compare the description of the slaughterhouse with a scene in one of the more graphic recent movies. The freewritings should open a discussion. At the same time, they should make students conscious of perhaps a double standard in their tolerance for blood and gore, which in turn could lead to an examination of the cultural and social reasons behind it. If, for some reason, these discussions stall, you can always ask for a comparison of this essay's structure with Naylor's and Fallow's, since they all use a form of narrative to get their point across. No matter which direction you go, this piece should be a springboard for a variety of writing topics.

Lewis Thomas, "The Art of Teaching Science"

Thomas leads into his conclusion by saying that "the worst thing that has happened to science education is that the fun has gone out of it." He's probably right; to verify this, begin class with a freewriting asking students to tell why they do or do not like science, or (without going into personalities) to tell about the best or worst science class they have ever had. Their responses should lead nicely into Thomas's quasi solutions. What are they? Divide students into groups and have them tell you. Once these solutions have been discovered and listed on the board, ask how concrete or useful they are. (They aren't.) Then let the students give concrete suggestions: What scientific issue or area would they like to know more about? What would be a good way to teach it? If you want to take this discussion further, have the class read Paolo Friere's "The Banking

Concept of Education" along with this piece. They can refer to Thomas's solutions and Friere's principles when discussing and designing potentially "fun" science units.

Joseph Epstein, "What Is Vulgar?"

Possibly the best way to open a class on this piece is to ask students to freewrite about what they think is gross or tacky and on what experiences they base their definitions. If you also do this exercise, you can compare your definitions with theirs to see whether there is a generation gap. This type of exercise gives students some practice in exploring their ideas while also giving them something to share with the class. The ensuing discussion can then relate their definitions to Epstein's. Whether they are the same or different, they will support his varied definitions, since he admits that what he thinks is vulgar is not the same as what others think. Once variety has been admitted, you can go a step further and ask students to respond to Epstein's statement that "there is even likable vulgarity" and ask for examples; or ask them to play the word association game he talks about and to quickly list "ten items you associate with the word 'vulgar.'" Either of these activities should get the students involved, keep them entertained, and help them learn about writing to explore.

Russell Baker, "Completely Different"

Reader response can help students see what is going on here. Ask them to freewrite about what they think the purpose of this piece is and on what they base their conclusions. You will probably get a variety of opinions. Before you start agreeing or disagreeing, distribute some ads that exemplify what Baker is talking about. Divide students into groups, give out one ad per group, and have each group decide how its ad illustrates or includes such elements as claims of "completely different"—without using any commas. Once they figure out Baker's purpose, ask why ads are like this. You can even bring in some ads from older magazines for comparison; then have students relate advertising to society, or discuss society's influence on the media, or vice versa.

ADDITIONAL WRITING ASSIGNMENTS

1. *Cultural differences.* Fallows, Naylor, Epstein, and Baker all touch on different conventions or cultural mores. Fallows implicity compares Japanese and American trash days; Naylor and Epstein look at how different words express one's place on the social ladder; Baker critiques the influence of advertising. All but Baker rely on varying degrees of narration to help them explore these ideas; all but Epstein also include comparisons. What societal or cultural issues bother you? Make a quick list of ten to twenty items. When you have finished, select two that have the most appeal, or about which you feel the strongest, and freewrite a page on each. From the fluency and detail of each freewriting, choose one to develop into a paper in which you explore your feelings on this subject. To help develop and illustrate your ideas, try using narration and comparison.

2.   *Education.* Thomas, Goodall, and Selzer (as well as Mellix, Mora, and O'Connor in earlier chapters) discuss their views of education and what it should and should not do. Have you ever explored your own feelings on what constitutes a good education or if you have received one? If this topic appeals to you, make a quick list of qualities a good education should instill in students. This list can be the basis of an essay exploring ideas about the quality of American education. Or it can serve as points of comparison. Make another list of what qualities you have actually gained during your schooling, and explore how these have helped or harmed you and your view of the world.

3.   *Animals.* Essays by Walker, Dillard, Sedgwick, Goodall, and Selzer have all dealt with the relationships between humans and animals and the human characteristics animals have, which we so often ignore. If you have had a similar experience, tell your story, using it as a frame to show what we can learn from supposedly "dumb" animals.

ANSWERS TO QUESTIONS

Goodall, "The Mind of the Chimpanzee"

1.   All of these topics are related to Goodall's implied thesis that the scientific community's narrow views of animals—as totally separate from human beings—blinds them and narrows the scope and possible insights of their research. Her anecdotes about Lucy show the chimp's "human" features, including emotions, while her discussion of scientific conventions shows how discussion of emotions is precluded.

2.   Goodall wants her readers to see the chimp's human traits.

3.   Scientists are reluctant to believe that animals have emotions, or even to discuss the possibility, because it is so difficult to prove. It is much easier to discuss human emotions because scientists can communicate verbally with their subjects and because they have experienced most of the same feelings.

4.   Goodall's lack of early training was an asset, because it freed her from the biases of scientific inquiry.

5.   Scientists snubbed her findings because Goodall talked about the animals' feelings. Her references to "trappings" and the "scientific ribbon" are alternative descriptions of scientific degrees and conventions.

6.   Goodall bases her claims upon years of observations. People might be afraid to take this approach because it is so "unscientific," since it goes beyond objective facts.

Fallows, "Land of Plenty"

1. Japanese life is very orderly; even the garbage is packaged neatly. Taking something home from the *sodai gomi* pile should be done discreetly. As Fallows notes in paragraph 9, it is also "important to give as well as receive."

2. Because the Japanese have small living areas and value "freshness and purity," most Japanese would probably find a garage sale either bewildering or repugnant. There seems to be an unwritten rule against buying secondhand goods.

3. Fallows waited until after midnight because he did not want anyone to see him raid the *sodai gomi* pile, since doing so went against cultural norms. At this point, he didn't yet know his neighbors. Paragraph 10 suggests that Fallows makes an effort to fit in.

4. Given what Fallows says about the Japanese "yen" for freshness and purity, they would not understand his piece. It is written for an American audience.

5. This essay defines an aspect of Japanese life as seen through the eyes of an American. In other words, it is a double definition. At the same time, it may have been written with a touch of irony, since Americans also throw away so much and yet are castigated as wasteful. The final scene seems also to exemplify Americans' competitive character, while leaving the essay on a humorous note.

Naylor, "Mommy, What Does 'Nigger' Mean?"

1. Naylor writes to make a living and to keep her sanity.

2. Naylor describes her family as "a large extended family that had migrated from the rural South after World War II and formed a close-knit network that gravitated around [her] maternal grandparents." She shows their interactions through dialogue, which helps explore the language issues this essay focuses on.

3. *Nigger* is described as a bad word, an insult, as "a man who had distinguished himself in some situation that brought . . . approval for his strength, intelligence or drive," as "a term of endearment for husband or boyfriend," "the pure essence of manhood," and, in the plural, people who lack self-respect. Context and inflection are necessary to understand the different meanings. Naylor could tell what the little boy meant by how he said it: he "spit out that word."

4. Some people might consider black usage of *nigger* to be internalization of racism because they believe only white racists use it—and always in a derogatory manner. Naylor sees its usage among her people as positive, because its many uses signified "the varied and complex human beings they knew themselves to be."

5. The last sentence shows the mother's need to explain racism in America and to comfort her against it.

Selzer, "How to Build a Slaughterhouse"

1. Selzer knows exactly how he feels about this slaughterhouse. Because of the amount of death he has seen there, he leaves wanting only to create life, "to make love."

2. Selzer visits to get a total view of how the slaughter is organized and how the slaughterhouse functions, so that he can adequately judge the students' abattoirs. But he also seems drawn by his own fascination with the scene.

3. The tulips *spurt*, like slit cows; the birds are *mourning* doves, appropriate for a scene involving death. The radio announcement is about famine, reminding readers that the world needs food and that concern for animals should not obscure other concerns. Compare Selzer's use of the dog with Orwell's use of the dog in "A Hanging."

4. Selzer seems to see the slitters as Machiavellian stars. Handsome yet sinister, they like their work. This is particularly evident when, in describing the second slitter, he describes the man's sudden laugh.

5. The efficiency is in their knives, whose blades glitter as they slice through the cows. The lack of feeling (or remorse) with which they do their jobs makes the killing seem wicked. I think Selzer wants to see some guilt, some acknowledgment that they are killing living things. But he is also dazzled by this well-organized process. He is by no means the first writer to find death fascinating or "glittering."

6. The architecture students are similar to the slaughterhouse workers in their blasé attitude toward killing and death. Selzer implies that the Yale residency program is brutal.

7. Selzer's ideal slaughterhouse provides an alternative, a more humane way of viewing life and death. Whether its omission would affect the impact of the essay depends upon the reader. Some might feel it provides relief; others might feel that nothing can take away the images of the real thing; still others might feel that it is unnecessary.

8. "Already the event is too far away for grief or pity. How quickly the horror recedes." His instructions to the butcher show how common it is for human beings to dismiss the slaughter of animals.

Thomas, "The Art of Teaching Science"

1. "Graduate schools blame the colleges; colleges blame the secondary schools; the high schools blame the elementary schools, which, in turn, blame the family." Thomas feels the scientific community is to blame.

2. Thomas believes science is mysterious because it is incomplete, and it is exciting because most accomplishments "are still in their very earliest stages." There are no firm, everlasting answers.

3. For students who are taught through lecture and tests, science will be excruciatingly boring; for those who are taught through experiment and application, it can be exciting. Too many students experience the former method (and not just in science); Thomas advocates the latter.

4. Since science touches everyone, everybody should know about it. If science is left to the scientists, it becomes interesting only to them and, in addition, gives them power over the nonscientists.

5. Thomas sees poets as deep thinkers, visionaries who see things differently and might "begin to see some meanings that elude the rest of us."

6. If Thomas wanted to use a straight argumentative form, the essay could become as dull as the science teaching he bemoans. An argument would also require Thomas to be more specific about how science education should be changed. By using an exploratory form, he is able to engage the attention of readers by stating the problem and speculating about solutions without commiting himself to developing a specific proposal.

Epstein, "What Is Vulgar"

1. Uncle Jake epitomizes what most people consider as vulgar behavior. By "outsized," Epstein means his uncle was larger than life.

2. Calling someone or something vulgar makes the caller feel self-righteous, better than someone else. Such presumption of superiority is vulgar.

3. The house is vulgar because it is ostentatious and tasteless, full of features that do not function but are designed only to elicit attention.

4. Epstein presents himself as an observer rather than a moral arbiter; he realizes that he has fun pointing out others' vulgarities and that he may have lapses of his own. Both incidents of forgetfulness occur in reference to the name of someone who called him vulgar. Forgetting their names shows how unimportant he considers them.

5. Epstein's phrasing suggests that people now go to great lengths to appear simple, so that, in contrast, elaborate ornamentation is easy.

6. Epstein uses the first half of the essay to establish that vulgar can be in the eye of the beholder and that everyone has been guilty of vulgarity and of damning others for it. If he had begun with a definition, these distinctions would not have been clear.

7. By understanding the meaning of *vulgar,* we can avoid becoming so and arrest what Epstein believes to be the decay of American culture.

Baker, "Completely Different"

1. Russell is looking at the language of advertising. The form and phrasing, with incomplete sentences and inadequate punctuation, mimic the form of ads. He is also exploring the American love of change and the shortness of many people's attention spans. The form emphasizes this as well.

2. The long sentences exemplify Mrs. Hummel, who is not a "new woman." Baker uses the first 49 paragraphs to establish a contrast of new from old.

3. The comma suggests a pause, which advertisers eschew as time-consuming. It also signals correct punctuation, something advertising also lacks. Its elimination eliminates pauses and correctness. Baker uses commas when quoting conversation—from real people—and when describing Mrs. Hummel, one of the few remaining real people.

4. Baker satirizes the language of advertising.

5. Baker finds the emphasis and lack of conventions in advertising to be changing the world for the worse.

CHAPTER 10

WRITING TO UNDERSTAND READING

As the authors point out in their introduction to this chapter, readers gain the most understanding of a text by writing about and responding to it. The notes in this manual give a variety of suggestions for writing and response. If you want to move beyond response and begin to prepare students for more formal writing, you can also have them experiment with the four modes most often associated with writing about literature: summary, review, explication, and analysis. Each reading lends itself to one or more of these modes.

Any one of the short stories or the play can be summarized in a journal entry. Comparison of these entries in class will help students fine-tune these skills. Any of the prose pieces can also be a subject for review, but you may want to assign this task to additional reading, such as a novel or play not in the textbook, since reviewing is most appropriate for these longer pieces. The poems are good choices for explication. Start the students with a short one so that they aren't intimidated. Once you see they understand the poetry, you can also have students do an evaluation by comparing two poems and determining which is the better.

Analysis is always the most difficult writing task, so it should be approached last. The earlier assignments asking students to read closely should prepare them to take something apart. They can analyze Oates's use of characterization, Mori's use of symbol, or Glaspell's use of scenes. If you have students do short, informal versions of these analyses—such as one or two pages freewritten in their journals—they will find the larger task of incorporating this analysis into a long paper less daunting.

But these assignments may not always be sufficient to aid the students' understanding. A variation on the dialogue used to develop argument in Chapter 5 can be applied here. Have students write a dialogue with the author of the piece. Since poetry often presents the most difficulty, you can have students address the author of any of the poems in this section. Another comprehension strategy is to divide the poem line by line and have each student "translate" it—put it into prose. Or you can change half a dozen words in the poem and then ask students to compare the two versions. These tactics not only make the poem clearer but also reinforce the qualities of preciseness and succinctness that poetry demands. That realization may lead to their increased respect for poetry.

To aid comprehension and recognition of the various elements of literature in this chapter, you can divide students into groups and have them analyze the short stories according to the elements of Burke's pentad. With five groups, each can describe one element of the pentad and then support the findings with examples and evidence from the piece. This type of exercise makes the entire story easier to follow; it can also teach students how to support and eventually document their evidence.

When each group has determined, for example, who the actor is within a short story and has found sufficient examples to support the findings, ask students to write their findings into a paragraph and to quote any material they take directly from the story. Then have each group explain the rules it followed for quoting text. This discussion will probably reveal some general or large-scale misunderstandings about the conventions of documentation, which in turn will set the stage for some explicit tips from you. These can be taught inductively or deductively. If you choose the latter, give the students some examples of correctly documented texts, ask them to generate rules for documentation, and then have them apply these rules to their own group work.

All of these exercises (plus the chapter notes, questions, and suggestions for writing) should provide adequate preparation for the students to write about literature. It should also have shown students their analytical strengths and weaknesses, so that they can decide whether to work with poetry or prose, and whether to summarize, analyze, explicate, or evaluate a literary text or to write a paper that includes a combination of these skills.

Even with this preparation, however, they will need to see models of literary essays. Telling them about the conventions and having them practice them on freewritten paragraphs is one thing; having them apply the conventions to an entire paper is a much larger task. They need to see how it's done. If you don't have any models from literature courses, you can find some in most of the newer texts on writing about literature. *Writing Essays about Literature* by Kelly Griffith, Jr., provides a number of useful examples. These models not only exemplify correct usage of conventions but also illustrate different modes of organization. For this very first literary paper, it wouldn't hurt to have students select a particular essay and use it as a model for organizing and developing their own. You can also direct students to the essays by Ruth Dorgan and Mark Twain in Chapter 8.

Of course, even with a model, students will still need to compose multiple drafts and get sufficient feedback so that they can revise. A literary paper follows essentially the same rules as a persuasive paper—it needs an engaging introduction, a clearly stated thesis, supporting examples, and logical organization that builds an argument and anticipates counterarguments. Pointing out these similarities to students may make this assignment easier for them; applying some of the same teaching strategies should make it easier for you.

Toshio Mori, "Abalone, Abalone, Abalone"

This is a very simple story, which is why it introduces this section. In its simplicity and layered meanings, it somewhat resembles a parable. If you are familiar with some parables, you can begin class by telling one or two, asking students to tell you any they recall and to explain what a parable is. Following this discussion, ask students to freewrite on whether Mori's story is a parable and what its message is. Parables are similar to allegories; one tells a story to make a moral or philosophical point, and the other uses fiction to make a point about human existence. To broaden the discussion, you can follow the same strategy with allegories—defining them, giving some examples, and having students freewrite about the story's purpose and allegorical properties. All of this writing should help students see beyond the basic narrative so that they begin to read critically.

Joyce Carol Oates, "Shopping"

The women in your class should be able to relate to this story easily, but the young men may not. They see the word *shopping* and immediately relegate the story to "female" topics—not for them. Of course, shopping and the mall are merely the setting. To get away from that and engage all the students, use reader response: Ask them to read the story and write about who they identify or sympathize with and why. (If you have the inevitable students who dislike both characters, have them write about the one they most dislike and tell why). This type of response gets the discussion into the dynamics of parent-child or adult-teen relationships and why they're so difficult. At the same time, it asks students to look closely at the details of the story to explain their preference. This strategy makes them more aware of the author's techniques—the use of action, dialogue, background, setting, and description to develop characterization. If not all of these are brought out in the discussion, ask students to list everything they know about mother and daughter and tell how they know it. This activity illustrates the intricacies of characterization, as well as Oates's skill in weaving the traits together.

Leslie Marmon Silko, "Lullaby"

It is difficult to guess how students will respond to this story. The good ones will appreciate the style, tone, and description; the poorer readers may get bogged down in the details. To elicit response, ask students to write about how the story made them feel and what details or incidents caused these feelings. They may feel angry at the white man, pity for Ayah, disgust with Chato, shame at the Indians' treatment. The type of response will vary with the reader's background. Listing their feelings and the details that evoked them can lead into a discussion of theme and tone and the relationship between the two. To clarify how these features can vary among authors—and, in fact, identify authors— divide students into small groups and ask them to compare the theme and tone of Silko and of Oates. This activity will help make students aware of the authors' varying techniques and help them recognize such strategies in other stories.

Garrett Hongo, "Off from Swing Shift"

You don't need to be told that students have trouble with poetry. They think it's weird, dense, hard, and tricky—there's always more to it than they can see on first reading. Hongo is an easy starting point because his poem is descriptive of a single character and involves little that is abstract. One way to get students past their fear and dread is to have them write a paraphrase of the poem following the reporter's five Ws—who, what, when, where, why? They should get the first four easily enough; then you can focus on the "why." In particular, why is this a poem? What distinguishes it from prose? Why did the author write it? What is his message? As with the other readings in this chapter, once students can answer these questions, you can ask them for specifics. Split them into groups, one per stanza, and have them pick out specific words or details that contribute to the poem's tone and message. This type of step-by-step analysis may make poetry easier for them to comprehend.

Gary Soto, "Black Hair"

You may want to assign Rodriguez's "Complexion" or Mora's "Letter to Gabriela" to set up a context for this poem; then ask students to freewrite about what the essay and this poem have in common. The similarities should be fairly obvious. From there, you can ask them why this piece is better as a poem, or what distinguishes it as such. As students discuss the word choices, images, and repetition—the concretization of a theme into a single poem—have them compare it with Hongo's. In groups, have students compare and contrast the two, looking for theme, purpose, and symbols. With the theme clear, you can have students write a similar poem. First, they can cluster ideas about a childhood hero and what he or she represented. Then working with those images, they can model their poem on Soto's, beginning stanza 1 with "At eight (or whatever age) I was . . ."; stanza 2 with "I came here because . . ."; and stanza 3 repeating the last part of line 1. When students see that they can crystallize an idea or memory into a poem, they will begin to better understand poetry's purpose.

William Shakespeare, Sonnet 116
and
Adrienne Rich, "Living in Sin"

These poems might best be taught by linking them together, since they show two different views of love, from different genders in different eras with different conventions. With this context in place, students should be better able to understand Shakespeare. Before they read, have students freewrite about who would write better love poems—men or women—and why. When they come to class, have them compare their freewriting to what they found in Rich and Shakespeare. Next, have them compare or contrast the two in a freewriting. What do they have in common? How are they different? Once the disparities are outlined, students can discuss the reasons for the differences—what role the conventions of the age play, or whether gender accounts for the greater difference. Depending on the students' responses, you might then bring in additional poems from the same era, by the opposite sex. It will be difficult to find any female contemporaries of Shakespeare. Elizabeth Barrett Browning and Emily Bronte are the first women anthologized; Emily Dickinson's tart poetry would also be a good contrast. Rich's male contemporaries are much easier to find, although they don't all focus on love. Theodore Roethke's "Wish for a Young Wife" is a short, accessible poem.

Alberto Rios, "Nani"
and
Audre Lorde, "Power"

Upon a first reading, these two poems seem to be total opposites. One is warm and regretful; the other is hot—harsh, angry, and powerful. Yet both writers are writing about alienation. This probably won't be immediately obvious to students. Have them begin by doing a freewriting on which poem they prefer, or which one moves them, and why. List each poem's characteristics on the board. This discussion should lead to a focus on word choice and images and show that what the author writes affects how the reader feels. But what adjectives describe what the author is feeling? As students begin to list descriptors, you can ask them who Lorde is angry at, or why Rios is sad. Such questions may lead to the realization that both poems reflect upon language and cultural differences even though they have radically different themes.

Alfred, Lord Tennyson, "Ulysses"
and
Gerard Manley Hopkins, "Pied Beauty"

Tennyson and Hopkins share a number of similarities: Both are nineteenth-century Englishmen (and, as such, firmly established in the canon, unlike several of the other writers selected for this chapter). Both are essentially upbeat. Assigning them after Hongo, Rich, Rios, and, especially, Lorde, will enable you to end a discussion of poetry on an affirmative note. Note also that both authors are much praised for the way they sound. At this point, assuming that students have attained a degree of comfort with poetry, you may want to ask some of the better students to read these poems aloud and have the rest of the class comment on the validity of this element of their reputation.

Susan Glaspell, *Trifles*

A good way to open a discussion of this play is to have students begin with a freewriting, telling whether or not Mrs. Wright is guilty and why. On the basis of their positions, divide the class in half. Further divide each half into groups, one group per reason, and have them prepare to debate their position, basing their arguments on evidence in the play. When each half has researched their arguments, have them appoint a leader to present the argument. You be the judge; list the arguments on the board, pro and con. On the basis of the amount of evidence gleaned from the play, you can arrive at a verdict. If the verdict is guilty, you and the class can decide on a sentence based on the circumstances. This type of activity should enable students to see how details and dialogue are used to shape plot, setting, and character and to judge their effectiveness. If you still have time left, have students do a freewriting on whether Mrs. Hale and Mrs. Peters are justified in concealing their discovery of the bird.

ADDITIONAL WRITING ASSIGNMENTS

1. *Symbols*. Mori, Hongo, Soto, Rios, Hopkins, and Glaspell use symbols to give their writing greater depth. Choose a poem, play, or short story and analyze its use of symbol. Show how the author frames and uses the symbol to make its significance clear.

2. *Characterization*. Oates, Silko, and Glaspell have written effectively because they are able to make their characters come alive through a combination of action, interaction, dialogue, and setting. Choose another short story, by one of these authors or by one of your choice, and write an analysis of the author's use of characterization.

3. *Poetry*. Each of the poets in this section uses poetry to convey a message or theme about a human experience. Through the use of word choice and images, they create a scene, a tone, a feeling. Depending on the author and the type of poetry you prefer, choose a poem and explain how the author uses language to create a mood or convey a message.

ANSWERS TO QUESTIONS

Mori, "Abalone, Abalone, Abalone"

1. At the beginning, the narrator seems to be a young boy, both because he refers to the abalone man as "Mr. Abe" and because Mr. Abe calls him "young man." At the beginning, he seems to be lonely but not very introspective. As the story progresses, the narrator remains lonely but begins to understand Mr. Abe's obsession with the shells. He begins to change when he finds and cleans his first abalone shell.

2. Mr. Abe probably feels he should not have to explain why he collects the shells; each person must discern and decide for himself. He doesn't plan to leave the shells to his children because they would not appreciate them. As the narrator illustrates, appreciation comes from one's own collection.

3. Apparently, polishing the shell is difficult because there are layers and layers of grime and various crevices that also must be cleaned. It is worth polishing because more and more luster and colors emerge. Compare this to what writers do when they revise their work, and direct students to the image on the book's cover, a picture that shows that hard work can reveal beauty beneath the mundane.

4. The sense of passing away, or moving on, is related to the idea of growth and change. One generation cannot necessarily pass on its knowledge to the next; each person must discover it independently, in his or her own way.

5.   The title is hard to understand even after reading the story. Using the word
     three times, each one separated from the next with a comma, suggests the
     sequence of collecting and the individuality of each shell.

Joyce Carol Oates, "Shopping"

1.   The first paragraph seems devoid of any emotion, "calm, neutral, free of
     irony," like Mrs. Dietrich. However, by the end of paragraph 2, the reader
     can sense Mrs. Dietrich's unhappiness through her hopes for increased
     intimacy, her desire for time alone with her daughter, and her sensitivity to
     Nola's silence. Note the weather: "a bleak March morning following a night
     of freezing rain, [with] a metallic cast to the air and no sun anywhere in the
     sky." Ask students why the light of this grey morning hurts Mrs. Dietrich's
     eyes.

2.   Mrs. Dietrich and Nola do not seem to have much to say to each other. The
     implication in paragraph 2 is that Nola does not particularly want to be
     doing this. At this point, their relationship seems typical of the ups and
     downs of mother-teenage daughter relationships: stormy, rocky, full of
     misunderstandings.

3.   The title appears to be innocuous, but it includes the setting and symbolizes
     Mrs. Dietrich's "shopping" for intimacy, as well as the idea that she can buy
     her daughter's love and companionship. Nola goes along to get the goods.
     They are relieved when they arrive because they can talk about impersonal
     objects.

4.   The woman in the black coat represents the other side of life—poor,
     homeless, without friends or family. She is Mrs. Dietrich without money. The
     shoppers, like most Americans, avoid her because they don't want to deal
     with her problem or admit she has one. Mrs. Dietrich's response typifies
     this attitude, whereas Nola's shows more empathy, although one wonders if
     she assumes this attitude simply to irritate her mother.

5.   We know that Mr. Dietrich has a good deal of money, that he betrayed his
     wife, that he's extremely critical and judgmental, that he was impatient with
     and did not try to understand his daughter's behavior. However, he used to
     be romantic.

6.   By calling her "Mrs. Dietrich," Oates characterizes her as a traditional
     woman defined by her husband's name (and money) and lacking an
     individual life or personality, as exemplified in her identifying with and
     clinging to her daughter.

7.   Nola wants to talk about the fact that she and her mother seem to have
     nothing in common, nothing to talk about.

8. Nola cries because she's sad—about life, about her lack of relationship with her mother, about society, about her inability to communicate her feelings in words.

Silko, "Lullaby"

1. The babies are gone; all she has is memories as she sits in the snow protected by an old woolen blanket.

2. Ayah seems attuned to nature. She does not find it threatening.

3. The government took her younger children because they said they had tuberculosis; Jimmy died in the war. The hardest loss was Jimmy because he was her firstborn son and because his death seemed so incomprehensible—he went away to war and just never came back.

4. Everything seems to revolve around Jimmy, possibly because his death was unresolved. He gave Ayah his blanket; he would have told her not to sign away the children; he could have helped his father work, so they would not have been turned out of their home.

5. "Maybe it was her face and the way she held her mouth with teeth clenched tight, like there was nothing anyone could do to her now." She is old and unattractive, repulsive in their eyes, but she has the strength and composure that comes from fearlessness and a clear sense of values.

6. The story shows that relations have never improved and that the two sides have never understood each other. Chato seemed to think that if he could speak English, he would be accepted, but Ayah is cynical.

7. The story has a somewhat ambiguous ending, since Ayah and Chato have been out all night before. But if they are freezing, it will be a relief, for she will be reunited with Jimmy and she and Chato will always be together.

Hongo, "Off from Swing Shift"

1. A swing shift runs from 3 to 11 P.M. The man is literally off work and away from the precise mechanical world of the job when he plays his games of chance. But he is also "off" in another sense. His life is less than it could be.

2. "Late" conjures up visions of dark night, after everyone has gone to bed, as well as tardiness, as if he didn't get home when he said he would. In this case, it also suggests a life that is too late for change.

3. Line 11 signals the break from work to home life, from drudgery to sports.

4. Within this context, "handicap" refers to an artificial advantage or disadvantage imposed on the horses to equalize the chances of winning. There can be "whole cosmologies" because of all the factors that can

influence a race, both figuratively and literally. In stanza 3, he plots "constellations" in the margins.

5. Repetition of "no one" suggests the isolation of the handicapped man.

6. While these names sound like some given to racehorses, they are also figurative reminders of the problems of his life.

Soto, "Black Hair"

1. At first glance, line 1 seems to contradict the image of a 50-pound stick of a boy, but that may be the point. He is "brilliant" with his body alone in his room before his baseball cards or sitting in the bleachers "waving players in and stomping [his] feet."

2. His primary reason for loving baseball is having Hispanic heroes to cheer on.

3. Hector Moreno is the boy's hero; he represents the possibility of accomplishment. Hector was the Trojan champion slain by Achilles; *hector* also means "to play the bully, to be arrogant or to swagger." This first name conjures up images of a swaggering ball player.

4. Apparently, the mother takes out her anger and grief—either figuratively or literally—on her children at the table. Help students see how people can be injured not only by sharp knives but also by dull and subtle weapons.

Shakespeare, Sonnet 116

1. The basis of true love is intellectual rather than physical. Note the last word in line 1.

2. Because of the phrasing, there seems to be some ambiguity in lines 1 and 2. *Admit* can mean either "acknowledge" or "allow to enter."

3. Time is like a sickle in that it cuts down lives, aging "rosy lips and cheeks." But according to Shakespeare, Time does not affect true Love.

4. The closing couplet affirms the truth of the first twelve lines by swearing that if he is wrong, then he has never written and "no man [has] ever loved." This is a pretty strong statement, which he knows is false.

Rich, "Living in Sin"

1. The poem is set in a dirty apartment. The woman had expected perfection, a picturesque setting. Phrases such as "last night's cheese and three sepulchral bottles" and "a pair of beetle-eyes" suggest the filth; "A plate of pears, a piano with a Persian shawl, a cat stalking the picturesque amusing mouse" show her expectations.

2. The steps actually creak, which means that the milkman's tramp is heavy. He comes every day, so he represents life going on and on in its sameness.

3. Minor demons are the different elements of the dirty apartment and a yawning lover; major ones would include death of love.

4. If by evening she is back in love "though not so wholly," it seems like each day she will love less because she will be worn down by the realities of life.

5. The title means literally that the couple is not married. The irony may come from the fact that living together doesn't measure up to expectations. What sounds romantic and possibly decadent is actually domestic and dreary. Note that very little "living" seems to be going on in this poem—the woman seems focused on simply enduring.

Rios, "Nani"

1. The speaker is younger than Nani and has become anglicized. He no longer is comfortable with his native language.

2. Spanish is used because these are Hispanic dishes, related to the speaker's renounced heritage. Spanish is not used more extensively because the poem is about the speaker's moving away from his native background and not owning the words he needs.

3. The speaker eats to please his grandmother. As the poem progresses, he seems to admit that he is full of heartache and confusion as well as food.

4. Possibly his last connection to his heritage will die with Nani.

5. Nani's loves and experiences are the steel that girds her; Rios uses the word *thing* because he doesn't seem able to put into words her love and his heritage that she represents.

Lorde, "Power"

1. Poetry has the power to kill internally, to kill the spirit when it doesn't work or won't come; rhetoric can be used to incite others or to justify indecent acts, such as an officer's killing a ten-year-old child.

2. The dead child in the dream represents the child the officer killed. The poem might lose some of its impact if the dream followed the account of the killing. Because the dream precedes the account, the reader is introduced to specific images of death, which make the real act all the more graphic and gruesome.

3. The policeman's words in stanza 3 reveal both his prejudice and his fear. The tapes are mentioned twice to illustrate the fact that despite evidence proving his guilt, the policeman was found innocent, thus illustrating the pervasive prejudice in this country.

4. The black woman on the jury was pressured to vote with the others because four centuries of white power had rendered her powerless and perhaps unable to believe in herself.

5. In line 18, the poet speaks of the "power of hatred and destruction"; in line 37, the black woman is pressured, in some ways by this same force, to "let go the first real power she ever had"—the power of her vote. In lines 41–43, the poet warns that "unless I learn to use/the difference between poetry and rhetoric/my power too will run corrupt." In other words, she must use her power for positive ends, in poetry, so that it does not turn into "hatred and destruction."

6. The speaker may not literally intend to rape an old woman, but her poem suggests that this is the degree of her anger and that of her race. The irony of the final line is that the racists are the beasts.

Tennyson, "Ulysses"

1. Ulysses is addressing the mariners who had accompanied him in the past. See lines 46–49 and 62–67.

2. He claims that he "cannot rest from travel" (6), but his decision is also influenced by his sense that Ithaca is unworthy of him. He wants to escape an "aged wife" (3) and a "savage race" (4) that fails to appreciate him. Lines 33–43 suggest that he also believes that he is, by temperament, unfit for the duties of kingship.

3. Experience is constantly unfolding; as long as we keep moving, we keep finding new horizons.

4. Ulysses claims that he loves his son, but his attitude seems patronizing. Describing Telemachus as "blameless" (39), Ulysses credits him with "slow prudence" (36) and says he is well suited for "common duties" (40). Recommending someone on the grounds that he is reliable suggests that there is nothing better one can say about him.

5. In line 62, Ulysses recognizes the possibility of being lost at sea. Lines 49–50, 65–67, and 69 show that Ulysses recognizes that he is old and that he does not have the strength he once enjoyed.

Hopkins, "Pied Beauty"

1. "Dappled things" are things with spots or things that are multicolored—in this poem, skies, rose-moles, chestnut leaves, finches' wings, landscapes. We should be thankful for them because they were all created by God.

2. "Pied Beauty" employs end rhyme in a pattern of *abc, abc, dbcdc*. There is also internal rhyme: rose-moles.

3. "Fathers-forth" means created. Beauty can be "past change" because since these things were created by God, they will always be beautiful.

4. The juxtapositions could be considered such—"swift, slow; sweet, sour; adazzle, dim." Note also how the poem's language is both original and compressed—as in lines 2–6—and that the last line stands apart.

Glaspell, *Trifles*

1. The kitchen is the heart of the house, where Mrs. Wright lived and worked, and is also the place where her canary was killed. This description of the kitchen makes it clear that Mrs. Wright had a grim life.

2. The most important act on stage is the women's discovery of the strangled bird. Off stage, Mrs. Wright has been psychologically abused, and she has retaliated by strangling her husband.

3. Their marriage was lonely and sad; it changed Mrs. Wright. The descriptions of how she used to be (singing like a bird) and of how Mr. Wright was (hard, not cheerful, close) show how he changed her.

4. The sheriff appears to be sexist, with no insight into a woman's point of view.

5. The response to this line changes as the conception of "trifles" changes. What men perceive as "trifles" may be more important than their own concerns.

6. They conceal the dead canary because they realize its death was Mrs. Wright's motivation for murder. They understand what the bird meant to her and wish to protect her.

7. The knots in the quilt parallel the knots Mrs. Wright apparently made to put a noose around her husband's neck. The men don't quite see this connection.

BIBLIOGRAPHY

Applebee, Arthur N. *Tradition and Reform in the Teaching of English: A History.* Urbana: NCTE, 1974.

Austin, J. L. *How to Do Things with Words.* Cambridge: Harvard UP, 1975.

Bartholomae, David. "Inventing the University." *When a Writer Can't Write: Studies in Writer's Block and Other Composing Process Problems.* Ed. Mike Rose. New York: Guilford, 1985. 134–65.

---. "The Study of Error." *College Composition and Communication* 31 (1980): 253–69.

Bazerman, Charles. "What Written Knowledge Does: Three Examples of Academic Discourse." *Philosophy of the Social Sciences* 11 (1981): 361–87.

Beach, Richard. "Self-Evaluation Strategies of Extensive Revisers and Nonrevisers." *College Composition and Communication* 27 (1976): 160–64.

Berlin, James. *Rhetoric and Reality.* Urbana: NCTE, 1987.

Berlin, James A., and Robert P. Inkster. "Current-Traditional Rhetoric: Paradigm and Practice." *Freshman English News* 8.3 (1980): 1+.

Berthoff, Ann E. *Forming/Thinking/Writing: The Composing Imagination.* Rochelle Park: Hayden, 1978.

---. "Is Teaching Still Possible? Writing, Meaning, and Higher Order Reasoning." *College English* 46 (1984): 743–55.

---. *The Making of Meaning: Metaphors, Models and Maxims for Writing Teachers.* Upper Montclair: Boynton/Cook, 1981.

---, ed. *Richards on Rhetoric: Selected Essays 1929–1974.* New York: Oxford UP, 1991.

Bizzell, Patricia. "Cognition, Convention, and Certainty: What We Need to Know about Writing." *Pre/Text* 3 (1982): 213–43.

---. "Marxism and Composition Studies." Paper delivered at the Conference on Composition and Literacy. University of San Francisco, June 1988.

---. "Thomas Kuhn, Scientism, and English Studies." *College English* 40 (1979): 764–71.

Bizzell, Patricia, and Bruce Herzberg, comps. *The Bedford Bibliography for Teachers of Writing.* New York: St. Martin's, 1991.

Bleich, David. *Readings and Feelings.* Urbana: NCTE, 1975.

Bloom, Lynn. *Fact and Artifact.* San Diego: Harcourt, 1985.

Booth, Wayne C. "The Rhetorical Stance." *College Composition and Communication* 14 (1963): 139–45.

Braddock, Richard. "The Frequency and Placement of Topic Sentences in Expository Prose." *Research in the Teaching of English* 8 (1974): 287–302.

Brannon, Lil. "Toward a Theory of Composition." *Perspectives on Research and Scholarship in Composition.* Ed. Ben W. McClelland and Timothy R. Donovan. New York: MLA, 1985. 6–25.

Brannon, Lil, Melinda Knight, and Vera Neverow-Turk. *Writers Writing.* Upper Montclair: Boynton/Cook, 1983.

Bridges, Charles W. "The Basics and the New Teacher in the College Composition Class." *Training the New Teacher of College Composition.* Ed. Charles W. Bridges. Urbana: NCTE, 1986. 13–26.

Britton, James, et al. *The Development of Writing Abilities (11–18).* London: Macmillan Education, 1975.

Bruffee, Kenneth A. "The Brooklyn Plan: Attaining Intellectual Growth through Peer-Group Tutoring." *Liberal Education* 64 (1978): 447–68.

---. "Collaborative Learning and the 'Conversation of Mankind.'" *College English* 46 (1984): 635–52.

---. "Social Construction, Language, and the Authority of Knowledge." *College English* 48 (1986): 773–90.

Bruton, Dawn L. and Dan R. Kirby. "Written Fluency: Didn't We Do That Last Year?" *English Journal* Nov. 1987: 89–92.

Burke, Kenneth. *A Grammar of Motives.* Berkeley: U of California P, 1969.

---. *A Rhetoric of Motives.* Berkeley: U of California P, 1969.

Chapman, David W. "Conflict and Consensus: How Composition Scholars View Their Discipline." *Profession* (1988): 43–45.

Christensen, Francis. "A Generative Rhetoric of the Sentence." *College Composition and Communication* 16 (1965): 144–56.

Coe, Richard M. "If Not to Narrow, Then How to Focus: Two Techniques for Focusing." *College Composition and Communication* 32 (1981): 272–77.

Coles, William E., Jr. *The Plural I: The Teaching of Writing.* New York: Holt, 1978.

Comprone, Joseph. "Kenneth Burke and the Teaching of Writing." *College Composition and Communication* 29 (1978): 336–40.

Corbett, Edward P. J. "Approaches to the Study of Style." *Twelve Bibliographic Essays.* Ed. Gary Tate and Edward P. J. Corbett. Fort Worth: Texas Christian UP, 1988. 83–130.

Crowley, Sharon. *A Teacher's Introduction to Deconstruction.* Urbana: NCTE, 1989.

Culler, Jonathan. *The Pursuit of Signs: Semiotics, Literature, Deconstruction.* Ithaca: Cornell UP, 1981.

D'Angelo, Frank J. "Literacy and Cognition: A Developmental Perspective." *Literacy for Life.* Ed. Richard W. Bailey and Robin Melanie Fosheim. New York: MLA, 1983. 97–114.

---. "Modes of Discourse." *Twelve Bibliographic Essays.* Ed. Gary Tate and Edward P. J. Corbett. Fort Worth: Texas Christian UP, 1988. 131–154.

Dillon, George L. *Constructing Texts.* Bloomington: Indiana UP, 1981.

Ede, Lisa. "Audience: An Introduction to Research." *College Composition and Communication* 35 (1984): 140–154.

Ede, Lisa, and Andrea Lunsford. "Audience Addressed/Audience Invoked: The Role of Audience in Composition Theory and Pedagogy." *College Composition and Communication* 35 (1984): 155–71.

Elbow, Peter. "Freewriting." *The Essay Connection.* Ed. Lynn Bloom. Heath: Boston, 1988. 30–33.

---. "Reflections on Academic Discourse." *College English* 53 (1991): 135–55.

Emig, Janet. *The Composing Processes of Twelfth Graders.* Urbana: NCTE, 1971.

---. "Hand, Eye, Brain: Some 'Basics' in the Writing Process." *Rhetoric and Composition: A Sourcebook for Teachers and Writers.* Ed. Richard Graves. Upper Montclair: Boynton/Cook, 1984. 359–70.

---. "Writing as a Mode of Learning." *College Composition and Communication* 28 (1977): 122–28.

Faigley, Lester. "Names in Search of a Concept: Maturity, Fluency, Complexity, and Growth in Written Syntax." *College Composition and Communication* 31 (1980): 291–300.

Faigley, Lester, Roger D. Cherry, David A. Joliffe, and Anna M. Skinner. *Assessing Writers: Knowledge and Processes of Composing.* Norwood: Ablex, 1985.

Faigley, Lester, and Stephen Witte. "Analyzing Revision." *College Composition and Communication* 32 (1981): 400–14.

Fish, Stanley. *Is There a Text in This Class?* Cambridge: Harvard UP, 1980.

Flower, Linda, and John R. Hayes. "The Cognition of Discovery: Defining a Rhetorical Problem." *College Composition and Communication* 31 (1980): 21–32.

Flower, Linda. "A Cognitive Process Theory of Writing." *College Composition and Communication* 32 (1981): 365–87.

---. "Writer-Based Prose: A Cognitive Basis for Problems in Writing." *College English* 41 (1979): 19–37.

Friere, Paolo. "The Banking Concept of Education." *Ways of Reading.* 2nd
    ed. Ed. David Bartholomae and Anthony Petrosky. New York: St. Martin's,
    1990. 206–18.

Fulwiler, Toby. "How Well Does Writing across the Curriculum Work?" *College
    English* 46 (1984): 113–25.

---. "Journal Writing across the Curriculum." *Classroom Practices in Teaching
    English, 1979–80: How to Handle the Paper Load.* Ed. G. Stanford.
    Urbana: NCTE, 1979. 15–22.

---. "Teaching Teachers to Teach Revision." *Revising: New Essays for Teachers
    of Writing.* Ed. Ronald A. Sudol. Urbana: NCTE, 1982. 100–109.

---. "Writing across the Curriculum: Implications for Teaching Literature." *ADE
    Bulletin* 88 (1987): 36–40.

Garrison, Roger H. "One-to-One: Tutorial Instruction in Freshman
    Composition." *New Directions for Community Colleges* 2 (1974): 55–84.

Geertz, Clifford. *Local Knowledge.* New York: Basic, 1983.

George, Diana. "Working with Peer Groups in the Composition Classroom."
    College Composition and Communication 35 (1984): 210–26.

Gorrell, Robert M. "How to Make Mulligan Stew: Process and Product Again."
    College Composition and Communication 34 (1983): 272–77.

Hairston, Maxine. "On Not Being a Composition Slave." *Training the New
    Teacher of College Composition.* Ed. Charles W. Bridges. Urbana: NCTE,
    1986. 117–124.

Harris, Joseph. "The Idea of Community in the Study of Writing." *College
    Composition and Communication* 40 (1989): 11–22.

Harris, Muriel. "The Overgraded Paper: Another Case of More Is Less."
    *Classroom Practices in Teaching English, 1979–80: How to Handle the
    Paper Load.* Ed. Gene Stanford. Urbana: NCTE, 1979. 91–94.

---. *Teaching One-to-One: The Writing Conference.* Urbana: NCTE, 1986.

Harris, Muriel, and Katherine E. Rowan. "Explaining Grammatical Concepts."
    Journal of Basic Writing 6 (1989): 21–41.

Hawkins, Thom. *Group Inquiry Practices.* Urbana: NCTE, 1976.

Heath, Shirley Brice. *Ways with Words: Language, Life and Work in
    Communities and Classrooms.* New York: Cambridge UP, 1983.

Kinneavy, James L. *Theory of Discourse.* New York: Norton, 1980.

Kinney, James. "Tagmemic Rhetoric: A Reconsideration." *College Composition
    and Communication* 29 (1978): 141–45.

Kline, Charles R., Jr., and W. Dean Memering. "Formal Fragments: The English
    Minor Sentence." *Rhetoric and Composition: A Sourcebook for Teachers
    and Writers.* Ed. Richard Graves. Upper Montclair: Boynton/Cook, 1984.
    148–61.

Kneupper, Charles W. "Revising the Tagmemic Heuristic: Theoretical and Pedagogical Considerations." *College Composition and Communication* 31 (1980): 160–67.

Knoblauch, C. H., and Lil Brannon. *Rhetorical Traditions and the Teaching of Writing.* Upper Montclair: Boynton/Cook, 1984.

Krashen, Stephen D. "What Is Known about Learning to Write." *Writing: Research, Theory, and Applications.* Oxford: Pergamon Institute of English, 1984. 4–19.

Kuhn, Thomas. *The Structure of Scientific Revolutions.* 2nd ed. Chicago: U of Chicago P, 1970.

Lakoff, George, and Mark Johnson. *Metaphors We Live By.* Chicago: U of Chicago P, 1980.

Lanham, Richard A. *Analyzing Prose.* New York: Scribner's, 1983.

Lindemann, Erika. *A Rhetoric for Writing Teachers.* New York: Oxford UP, 1987.

Lunsford, Andrea A. "The Content of Basic Writers' Essays." *College Composition and Communication* 31 (1980): 278–90.

Miller, Susan. "What Does It Mean to Be Able to Write? The Question of Writing in the Discourses of Literature and Composition." *College English* 45 (1983): 219–35.

Moffett, James. *Teaching the Universe of Discourse.* Boston: Houghton, 1968.

Murray, Donald. "Internal Revision." *Learning by Teaching.* Montclair: Boynton/Cook, 1982.

---. "Teaching Writing as Process, Not Product." *Learning by Teaching.* Montclair: Boynton/Cook, 1982.

---. "Write Before Writing." *College Composition and Communication* 29 (1978): 375–81.

---. "Writing as Process: How Writing Finds Its Own Meaning." *Eight Approaches to Teaching Composition.* Ed. Timothy R. Donovan and Ben W. McClelland. Urbana: NCTE, 1980. 3–20.

Neel, Jasper. *Plato, Derrida, and Writing.* Carbondale: Southern Illinois UP, 1988.

Ohmann, Richard. "Use Definite, Specific, Concrete Language." *College English* 41 (1979): 390–97.

Ong, Walter J. "The Writer's Audience Is Always a Fiction." *PMLA* 90 (1975): 9–21.

Perelman, Chaim. *The Realm of Rhetoric.* Trans. William Kuback. 1977. Notre Dame: U of Notre Dame P, 1982.

Perelman, Chaim, and Lucie Olbrechts-Tyteca. *The New Rhetoric: A Treatise on Argumentation.* Notre Dame: U of Notre Dame P, 1969.

Perry, William G., Jr. *Intellectual and Ethical Development in the College Years: A Scheme.* New York: Holt, 1970.

Petrosky, Anthony R. "From Story to Essay: Reading and Writing." *College Composition and Communication* 33 (1982): 19–36.

Pfister, Fred R., and Joanne F. Petrick. "A Heuristic Model for Creating a Writer's Audience." *College Composition and Communication* 29 (1979): 213–220.

Piaget, Jean. *The Language and Thought of the Child.* 1926. New York: World, 1955.

Reagan, Sally Barr. "Less Is More: Engaging Students in Learning." *Journal of Teaching Writing* 8 (1989): 41–50.

---. "Teaching Reading in the Writing Classroom." *Journal of Teaching Writing* 5 (1986): 177–85.

Rorty, Richard. *Philosophy and the Mirror of Nature.* Princeton: Princeton UP, 1979.

Rose, Mike. "Rigid Rules, Inflexible Plans, and the Stifling of Language: A Cognitivist Analysis of Writer's Block." *College Composition and Communication* 32 (1981): 389–401.

---, ed. *When a Writer Can't Write: Studies in Writer's Block and Other Composing Process Problems.* New York: Guilford, 1985.

Schwartz, Mimi, ed. *Writer's Craft, Teacher's Art: Teaching What We Know.* Portsmouth: Boynton/Cook, 1991.

Scott, Robert L. "Chaim Perelman: Persona and Accommodation in the New Rhetoric." *Pre/text* 5 (1984): 89–95.

Smith, Frank. *Writing and the Writer.* New York: Random, 1982.

Sommers, Nancy. "Revision Strategies of Student Writers and Experienced Adult Writers." *College Composition and Communication* 32 (1981): 378–388.

Toulmin, Stephen. *The Uses of Argument.* New York: Cambridge UP, 1964.

Trimbur, John. "Collaborative Learning and Teaching Writing." *Perspectives on Research and Scholarship in Composition.* Ed. B. W. McClelland and T. R. Donovan. New York: MLA, 1985. 87–110.

Vygotsky, Lev. *Thought and Language.* Trans. Eugenia Hanfman and Gertrude Vakar. Cambridge: MIT, 1962.

Walvoord, Barbara E. Fassler. *Helping Students Write Well: A Guide for Teachers in All Disciplines.* New York: MLA, 1982.

Weaver, Constance. "Parallels between New Paradigms in Science and in Reading and Literary Theories: An Essay Review." *Research in the Teaching of English* 19 (1985): 298–316.

White, Edward M. "Post-Structural Literary Criticism and the Response to Student Writing." *College Composition and Communication* 35 (1984): 186–95.

---. *Teaching and Assessing Writing*. San Francisco and London: Jossey-Bass, 1985.

Williams, Joseph M. "The Phenomenology of Error." *College Composition and Communication* 32 (1981): 151–68.

---. *Style: Ten Lessons in Clarity and Grace*. 3rd ed. New York: HarperCollins, 1989.

Winterowd, Ross. "The Grammar of Coherence." *College English* 31 (1970): 328–35.

Witte, Stephen P., and Lester Faigley. "Coherence, Cohesion, and Writing Quality." *College Composition and Communication* 32 (1981): 189–204.

Zeni, Jane. "Journals—Write More, Grade Less." *Classroom Practices in Teaching English, 1979–80: How to Handle the Paper Load*. Ed. G. Stanford. Urbana: NCTE, 1979. 9–14.

SUGGESTED READINGS

CHAPTER 1

Berg, Allison, J. Kowaleski, C. LeGuin, E. Weinauer, and E. Wolfe. "Breaking the Silence." *Feminist Teacher* 4 (1989): 29–32.

Bleich, David. "Homophobia and Sexism as Popular Values." *Feminist Teacher* 4: (1989): 21–28.

Elbow, Peter. "Freewriting." *The Essay Connection.* Ed. Lynn Bloom. San Diego: Harcourt, 1988. 30–33.

Fulwiler, Toby. "Journal Writing across the Curriculum." *Classroom Practices in Teaching English, 1979–80: How to Handle the Paper Load.* Ed. G. Stanford. Urbana: NCTE, 1979. 15–22.

---. "Responding to Student Journals." *Writing and Response.* Ed. C. Anson. Urbana: NCTE, 1989. 149–173.

Olney, James, ed. *Autobiography: Essays Theoretical and Critical.* Princeton: Princeton UP, 1980.

Sanders, Scott Russell. "The Singular First Person." *Sewanee Review* 96 (1988): 658–72.

Zeni, Jane. "Journals—Write More, Grade Less." *Classroom Practices in Teaching English, 1979–80: How to Handle the Paper Load.* Ed. G. Stanford. Urbana: NCTE, 1979. 9–14.

CHAPTER 2

Catano, James V. "The Rhetoric of Masculinity: Origins, Institutions, and the Myth of the Self-Made Man." *College English* 52 (1990): 421–36.

Clarke, Suzanne. "Annie Dillard: The Woman in Nature and the Subject of Nonfiction." *Literary Nonfiction: Theory, Criticism, Pedagogy.* Ed. Chris Anderson. Carbondale: Southern Illinois UP, 1989. 107–24.

Didion, Joan. *Slouching Towards Bethlehem.* New York: Farrar, 1968.

Dillard, Annie. *Pilgrim at Tinker Creek.* New York: Harper's Magazine P, 1974.

Emig, Janet. "Writing as a Mode of Learning." *College Composition and Communication* 28 (1977): 122–28.

Flynn, Elizabeth. "Composing as a Woman." College Composition and Communication 39 (1988): 423–35.

Hall, Michael L. "The Emergence of the Essay and the Idea of Discovery." *Essays on the Essay: Redefining the Genre*. Ed. Alexander J. Butrym. Athens: U of Georgia P, 1989. 73–91.

Rodriguez, Richard. *Hunger of Memory: The Education of Richard Rodriguez*. Boston: Godine, 1982.

CHAPTER 3

Allen, Woody. *Side Effects*. New York: Ballantine, 1980.

Aristotle. *Poetics*. Trans. Ingram Bywater. New York: Mod. Lib., 1954.

---. *Rhetoric*. Trans. Rhys Roberts. New York: Mod. Lib., 1954.

Bakhtin, Mikhail. *Rabelais and His World*. Trans. Helene Swolsky. Bloomington: Indiana UP. 1984.

Bergson, Henri. "Laughter." Rpt. in *Comedy*. Ed. Wylie Sypher. New York: Doubleday, 1957.

Vernon, Enid, ed. *Humor in America*. New York: Harcourt, 1971.

CHAPTER 4

Blair, Hugh. Lecture XXXII. *Lectures on Rhetoric and Belles Lettres*. Ed. Harold F. Harding. Carbondale: Southern Illinois UP, 1965.

Litwack, Leon. *Been in the Storm So Long: The Aftermath of Slavery*. New York: Knopf, 1979.

Miller, Keith. "Martin Luther King, Jr., Borrows a Revolution: Argument, Audience, and Implications of a Secondhand Universe." *College English* 48 (1986): 249–65.

Rackham, Jeff, and Olivia Bertagnolli. *From Sight to Insight*. 3rd ed. New York: Holt, Chapter 20, "Imaginative Leads." 203–11.

CHAPTER 5

Aristotle. *Rhetoric*. Trans. Rhys Roberts. New York: Mod. Lib., 1954.

Burke, Kenneth. *A Rhetoric of Motives*. Berkeley: U of California P, 1969.

Cicero. *Of Oratory*. Book II. Trans. E. W. Sutton and H. Rackham. Loeb Classical Library. Cambridge: Harvard UP, 1967.

Kneupper, Charles W. "Teaching Argument: An Introduction to the Toulmin Model." *College Composition and Communication* 29 (1978): 237–41.

---. "The Tyranny of Logic and the Freedom of Argumentation." *Pre/text* 5 (1984): 113–21.

Perelman, Chaim. *The New Rhetoric and the Humanities: Essays in Rhetoric and Its Applications.* Dordrecht: Reidel, 1980.

Quintilian. *Institutio Oratoria.* Trans. H. E. Butler. 4 vols. Loeb Classical Library. Cambridge: Harvard UP, 1959–63.

Toulmin, Stephen. *The Uses of Argument.* New York: Cambridge UP, 1964.

CHAPTER 6

Kaye, Elizabeth. "Growing Up Stoned." *Themes in Variation.* Ed. W. Ross Winterowd and Charlotte Preston. San Diego: Harcourt, 1985. 206–22.

Kinneavy, James L. *Theory of Discourse.* New York: Norton, 1980. Chapter 3: "Reference Discourse." 89–96.

Macrorie, Ken. *Telling Writing.* Rochelle Park: Hayden, 1970.

Mathis, J. C., and Dwight W. Stevenson. *Designing Technical Reports.* 2nd ed. New York: Macmillan, 1991. 243–79.

Oliu, Walter E., Charles T. Brusaw, and Gerald J. Allred. "Conducting Yourself Well During the Interview." *Writing That Works.* 3rd ed. New York: St. Martin's, 1988. 439–44.

Spatt, Brenda. *Writing from Sources.* 2nd ed. New York: St. Martin's, 1987.

CHAPTER 7

Chittick, Roger D., and Robert D. Stevick. *Rhetoric for Exposition.* New York: Appleton, 1961.

Grice, H. P. "Logic and Conversation." *The Logic of Grammar* Ed. Donald Davidson and Gilbert Harman. Encino: Dickinson Publ. Co., 1975. 64–153.

Huckin, Thomas N. "A Cognitive Approach to Readability." *New Essays in Technical and Scientific Communication: Research, Theory, Practice.* Ed. P. V. Anderson, R. J. Brockmann, and C. R. Miller. Farmingdale: Baywood, 1983. 90–108.

Kinneavy, James. *Theory of Discourse.* New York: Norton, 1980. Chapter 3: "Reference Discourse." 77–86.

Martin, Harold C., and Richard M. Ohmann. *The Logic and Rhetoric of Exposition.* New York: Holt, 1963.

Mitford, Jessica. *The American Way of Death.* New York: Simon, 1963.

Smith, Frank. "Twelve Easy Ways to Make Reading Difficult, and One Difficult Way to Make It Easy." *Psycholinguistics and Reading.* Ed. Frank Smith. New York: Holt, 1973. 183–96.

CHAPTER 8

Bloom, Lynn. *Fact and Artifact.* San Diego: Harcourt, 1985. "Writing about Performance." 159–91.

Brooks, Cleanth, R. W. B. Lewis, and Robert Penn Warren, eds. "Walt Whitman." *American Literature: The Makers and the Making, 1826–1861.* New York: St. Martin's, 1973.

Guilford, Chuck. "Creating a Learning Flow for Exploratory Writing." *College Composition and Communication* 41 (1990): 460–65.

Twain, Mark. *Selected Shorter Writings of Mark Twain.* Ed. Walter Blair. Boston: Houghton, 1962.

Whitman, Walt. *Leaves of Grass.* Ed. Harold W. Blodgett and Sculley Bradley. New York: New York UP, 1965.

CHAPTER 9

Epstein, Joseph. *Plausible Prejudices: Essays on American Writing.* New York: Norton, 1985. "Piece Work: Writing the Essay." 397–411.

Friere, Paolo. *The Pedagogy of the Oppressed.* New York: Seabury, 1973.

Kinneavy, James. *Theory of Discourse.* New York: Norton, 1980. Chapter 3: "Reference Discourse." 96–106.

Schuster, Charles. "The Nonfictional Prose of Richard Selzer." *Literary Nonfiction: Theory, Criticisms, Pedagogy.* Ed. Chris Anderson. Carbondale: Southern Illinois UP, 1989. 3–28.

Tompkins, Jane. "Fighting Words: Unlearning to Write the Critical Essay." *Georgia Review* 42 (1988): 585–90.

Zeiger, William. "The Exploratory Essay: Enfranchising the Spirit of Inquiry in College Composition." *College English* 47 (1985): 454–66.

CHAPTER 10

Gibaldi, Joseph and Walter S. Achtert. *MLA Handbook for Writers of Research Papers.* 3rd ed. New York: MLA, 1988.

Griffith, Kelly, Jr. *Writing Essays about Literature.* San Diego: Harcourt, 1982.

Kahn, Elizabeth, Carolyn C. Walter, and Larry R. Johannessen. *Writing about Literature.* Urbana: ERIC/RCS and NCTE, 1984.

MacAllister, Joyce. *Writing about Literature.* New York, Macmillan, 1987.

Martin, Bruce K. "Teaching Literature as Experience." *College English* 51 (1989): 377–86.

Williams, Nancy Cervetti, and Scott Cawelti, eds. *Literary Theory in the Classroom.* Urbana: NCTE, 1989.